TRADE LIBERALISATION AND THE ENVIRONMENT

TRADE LIBERALISATION AND THE ENVIRONMENT

A Computable General Equilibrium Analysis

Blair Townsend

Ravi Ratnayake

University of Auckland

World Scientific

Singapore • New Jersey • London • Hong Kong

Published by

World Scientific Publishing Co. Pte. Ltd.
P O Box 128, Farrer Road, Singapore 912805
USA office: Suite 1B, 1060 Main Street, River Edge, NJ 07661
UK office: 57 Shelton Street, Covent Garden, London WC2H 9HE

Library of Congress Cataloging-in-Publication Data
Townsend, Blair.
Trade liberalisation and the environment : a computable general equilibrium analysis / Blair Townsend, Ravi Ratnayake.
p. cm.
Includes bibliographical references.
ISBN 9810241941 (alk. paper)
1. Free trade--Environmental aspects--New Zealand. 2. Environmental policy--New Zealand. 3. New Zealand--Commercial policy. I. Ratnayake, Ravi. II. Title.

HF2570.5.T68 2000
333.7'0993--dc21 00--043317

British Library Cataloguing-in-Publication Data
A catalogue record for this book is available from the British Library.

Printed in Singapore by FuIsland Offset Printing

— Contents —

— List of Tables —

— *List of Figures* —

— Abbreviations —

APEC	Asia-Pacific Economic Co-operation
CBD	Convention on Biological Diversity
CER	Closer Economic Relations
CES	Constant Elasticity of Substitution
CFC	Chlorofluorocarbon
CGE	Computable General Equilibrium
CNG	Compressed Natural Gas
CO_2	Carbon Dioxide
CRS	Constant Returns to Scale
DoC	Department of Conservation
EC	European Community
ECC	Environmental Control Costs
EECA	Energy Efficiency Conservation Authority
FAO	Food and Agriculture Organisation of the United Nations
FCCC	Framework Convention on Climate Change
GAMS	General Algebraic Modelling System
GATT	General Agreement on Tariffs and Trade
Gg	Gigagrams (= million tonnes)
IEA	International Energy Agency
IPCC	Intergovernmental Panel on Climate Change
ISO	International Standards Organisation
LES	Linear Expenditure System

LPG	Liquid Petroleum Gas
MAF	Ministry of Agriculture and Fisheries
MFAT	Ministry of Foreign Affairs and Trade
MfE	Ministry for the Environment
MoC	Ministry of Commerce
NAFTA	North American Free Trade Agreement
NGO	Non-Governmental Organisation
OECD	Organisation for Economic Co-operation and Development
PECC	Pacific Economic Co-operation Council
PPP	Polluter Pays Principle
QMS	Quota Management System
RCA	Revealed Comparative Advantage
RMA	Resource Management Act
SMP	Supplementary Minimum Price
SOE	State-Owned-Enterprise
TCC	Tradable Carbon Certificate
UN	United Nations
UNCED	United Nations Conference on the Environment and Development
UNCTAD	United Nations Conference on Trade and Development
UNEP	United Nations Environment Programme
WTO	World Trade Organisation

— Chapter 1 —

Introduction

Issues in Trade and Environment

The last few years have seen a substantial increase in environmental concerns, as well as considerable greening of world politics. The number and scope of environmental concerns are growing rapidly and intensifying public interest in environmental issues. These concerns have raised the fear that irreversible damage is being done to the planet through the exhaustion of finite natural resources, the reduction in biodiversity and the continued pollution of air, land and water resources. One particular focus of these concerns is the interaction between international trade and the environment.

The environmental community argues that free trade is partly responsible for environmental problems because free trade is likely to increase production and consumption of environmentally unfriendly goods and services leading to high pollution and environmental degradation. On the one hand, trade policy instruments such as import bans and export taxes have been suggested to minimise the damage caused by such trade. On the other hand, environmental measures such as eco-labelling schemes, recycling programmes, and environmental certification schemes are being increasingly applied to products according to their environmental impact over their entire life cycle (including production use and disposal). This is because damage to the environment is increasingly seen as the result of the production process or disposal of products, with some of this damage occurring on a global scale (e.g. ozone depletion and global warming). Consequently, environmental regulations and standards have tended more recently to be applied to the production process rather than to the end-product, and have begun to have a much larger impact on international trade (Hewison, 1995). A well-known example is the United States Marine Mammal Protection Act which requires all Tuna sold in the United States, whether produced domestically or imported, to be caught using fishing methods that do not kill excessive numbers of dolphins. This type of environmental measure is in direct conflict with international trading rules, which provide that similar or like products cannot be discriminated against on the basis of how or where they were produced, and as such, the GATT Dispute Panel ruled the above regulation in contravention of international trade rules.

Increasing economic openness has led to concerns about possible detrimental effects on the environment. Expanded trading opportunities in natural resources and hazardous products, the possibility that trade liberalisation can significantly undercut domestic environmental policies through trade diversion, and relocation of dirty industries to "pollution havens", have augmented fears about the environment. At the same time, pressures have mounted to use trade instruments to achieve environmental ends. There is an emerging consensus in the environmentalist community opposing free trade (Drake-Brockman & Anderson, 1994). While some economists see this as merely another excuse for protectionism, recent work involving the investigation of theoretical and empirical relationships between international trade and environmental quality has begun. The recent greening of world politics has brought forward many claims as to the effects of trade and hence trade policy on the environment. Environmentalists have also made suggestions for government intervention to slow the degradation of the natural environment, which will not only affect the implementing country but also the trade, environment and welfare of other countries as well.

Supporters of free trade argue that international trade generates gains from specialisation and exchange to the countries involved in such trade and that the additional income received can be used for protecting the environment. Furthermore, they argue that trade restrictions do not attack the underlying causes of environmental problems and that the domestic environmental measures such as pollution taxes, charges and standards are more effective than trade measures.

Supporters of trade liberalisation and environmental protection share a common goal, to improve social welfare, and a common problem, the need to promote multilateral co-operation to fully achieve that objective. However, environmentalists tend to see trade policy as merely a potential instrument to achieve their objectives (either to "compensate" domestic producers for high domestic environmental standards or to entice other countries to raise their environmental standards) (Drake-Brockman & Anderson, 1994). A few environmentalists even see trade as part of the problem of global environmental degradation as they believe it accelerates growth and that this promotes pollutive activities and speeds the depletion of non-renewable resources. Supporters of international trade argue that multilateral harmonisation and mutual recognition of environmental measures and the establishment of international rules by which to judge these national measures must be introduced to further the expansion of world trade. Many environmentalists and public interest groups are concerned however, that in some cases these efforts will compromise other measures taken to protect the environment and in turn will either lead to the lowering of standards or undermine future attempts to raise standards, as well as remove decision-making from the national to the international level (where it is more difficult and expensive for them to assert any influence).

Free traders tend to take exception to the environmentalists impinging into the free trade debate, especially when they believe that freer trade is environmentally friendly, not only in the sense that it allows more efficient allocation of the world's resources, but also in the sense that by raising living standards it enables a greater allocation of resources to protecting the environment. It is postulated that international trade may have both positive and negative effects on the environment depending on a number of factors including, the existence of optimal environmental protection measures, how property rights are defined, the level of economic and technological development and the level of environmental awareness and preferences concerning the environment.

In most sectors the direct effects of trade are small, largely due to the fact that only a small share of environmentally-sensitive goods are traded and because trade is only one of many factors that affect the environment. Less well understood are the indirect effects trade may have on the environment through its influence on world prices and market conditions. In general, trade is not the fundamental cause of environmental problems, which are predominantly the result of market and intervention failures (OECD, 1994a). Market failures result from the inability of the market to correctly value and allocate environmental resources and the failure to internalise environmental costs in commodity prices. Intervention failures occur when government policies (environmental, trade and others) do not correct for, create, or exacerbate market failures. Trade expands the scale of economic activity and market growth, which can provide additional resources for environmental protection, but which may also be environmentally detrimental in the presence of market and intervention failures. Trade also facilitates the international diffusion of environmentally beneficial products and services, but similarly it is also the means by which environmentally harmful goods are exchanged internationally. More indirectly, the effects of trade on the global allocation of production and consumption can have either positive or negative environmental effects dependant largely on the presence of appropriate environmental policies. Less is known about the impacts of trade liberalisation on the environment. Trade liberalisation should have significant positive effects on the environment, particularly in correcting trade policy intervention failures that are presently environmentally harmful. Trade liberalisation may also have some negative impacts, which in general are a result of trade expansion in the absence of correcting other market and intervention failures.

Three significant trade consequences of the greening of world politics have emerged during recent years. In 1992 at the United Nations Conference on Environment and Development (UNCED) in Rio de Janeiro, a comprehensive set of issues known as Agenda 21 was identified requiring international co-operation in the pursuit of sustainable development. In Chapter 2 of Agenda 21, a trade and environment programme was decided, and this has subsequently been pursued in a number of international organisations, such as the OECD (Organisation for Economic Co-operation and Development), UNCTAD (United Nations Conference on Trade and

Development) and UNEP (United Nations Environment Programme) as well as the GATT (General Agreement on Tariffs and Trade). In 1993, the OECD produced a set of guidelines for trade and environment policy, designed to encourage OECD member governments to work towards making national trade and environmental policies more mutually compatible and supportive.

The second followed the conclusion of the Uruguay Round of Multilateral Trade Negotiations at Marrakesh in April 1994, where Contracting Parties agreed to establish the World Trade Organisation (WTO) to supersede the GATT. The Preamble to the agreement establishing the WTO refers to its objective as:

> Expanding the production and trade in goods and services, while allowing for the optimal use of the world's resources in accordance with the objective of sustainable development, seeking both to protect and preserve the environment and enhance the means for doing so in a manner consistent with their respective needs and concerns at different levels of economic development.[1]

A GATT/WTO Committee on Trade and Environment was also established to ensure that trade rules are responsive to environmental objectives by co-ordinating trade and environmental policies within the multilateral trading system.

Thirdly, the 1993 signing of an environmental side agreement to the North American Free Trade Agreement (NAFTA) set an international precedent. That precedent, when combined with the fact that the OECD countries agreed to subject trade agreements and trade policies to environmental review as a part of the OECD guidelines on trade and environment, tends to suggest that future trade reforms by NAFTA countries will incorporate policies to manage environmental concerns.

There is little doubt this greening of world politics has the potential to improve global welfare. Liberalisation and expansion of international trade and growth and protection of the natural environment are all compatible with the concept of sustainable development. There is however the possibility

[1]Drake-Brockmanm & Anderson (1994).

that certain restrictive trade policies, adopted in response to environmental concerns, are sufficiently inefficient so as to worsen welfare in many countries. Furthermore, these restrictive trade policies in some cases may even heighten rather than reduce environmental degradation. As such, there is a demand for an improved understanding of the various interactions between trade and the environment, and between environmental and trade policies, as well as their respective effects on welfare.

New Zealand as a Case Study

There has also been a recent intensification of interest in environmental matters in New Zealand which has, in conjunction with New Zealand's reliance on environmental quality to maintain it's international "clean-green" image, raised the profile of the trade and environment debate in New Zealand. An article in *New Scientist* entitled "New Zealand's Poisoned Paradise" on contaminated waste timber treatment sites and the OECD's call for co-ordinated trade and environment policies has further strengthened the emphasis on trade and environment policy issues in New Zealand. These issues are of particular relevance for New Zealand because of its dependence on international trade, and the removal of trade-related protectionist measures. Growth in the New Zealand economy has been predicated on economy-wide reforms, in particular trade and investment liberalisation, and this trend towards a more open and deregulated economy is forecasted to continue (Hewison, 1995). Environmentalism is now a significant influence on public policy development in New Zealand as in other countries and is likely to continue to increase in importance. In response to these increasing environmental concerns New Zealand has recently introduced innovative environmental policies which promote sustainability. Furthermore, New Zealand is expected to implement additional environmental policies in the near future such as a carbon tax to limit carbon dioxide emissions.[2] These factors, combined with the present lack of trade- and environment-related

[2]See MfE (1994) and Working Group on CO_2 Policy (1996).

studies on New Zealand, mean that an investigation of the likely effects of trade liberalisation on welfare and carbon dioxide emissions, both in the absence and presence of a carbon tax, is particularly pertinent.

The analysis of New Zealand in this study also offers another advantage. Being a small open market-based economy, the results following from the investigation of the effects of trade liberalisation on the environment and welfare will be widely applicable to other similar economies. This can easily be seen, for example, in the case of APEC (Asia-Pacific Economic Co-operation) members, where many of the economies are also small and as such, the majority of the assumptions employed throughout this study remain appropriate. Furthermore, the application of the results from this study to other APEC economies is particularly relevant given their commitment to ongoing trade liberalisation within the "open regionalism" ideology. Growth within the Asia-Pacific region has been founded on ongoing liberalisation of the multilateral trading system, and of the trade and investment regimes of member countries (Drake-Brockman & Anderson, 1994). As such, the movement towards greater environmental protection and the increasing interest in the environmental effects of trade liberalisation is deserving of attention as these economies commit to more liberalised trade regimes. Furthermore, as the profile of the environment increases, there is the risk that if the environmental effects of trade liberalisation are not adequately addressed, then the present commitment to ongoing liberalisation may be jeopardised. Therefore, the analysis of these effects for New Zealand and the resultant policy implications will be of value to other small market-based economies contemplating liberalisation of their trade regimes.

Objectives of the Study

This study attempts to assess the magnitude of the effects of trade liberalisation on welfare and emissions levels in the New Zealand economy, and the degree to which these effects are influenced by environmental policy. It is expected that the results of this study will be able to provide some direction for New Zealand's trade and environmental policies and should help to fill some of the empirical vacuum in this field. Although this study concentrates on the effects within the New Zealand economy, the results subsequently obtained will be widely applicable to other small open market-based economies. Based on theoretical analyses, it is anticipated that the results will show trade liberalisation to be welfare-enhancing in the presence of environmental policies that internalise environmental externalities. As the questions raised in this study have economy-wide implications, this study assesses the consequences of trade and environmental policies by incorporating a trade and environment focus into a computable general equilibrium (CGE) model for the New Zealand economy. This question is easily examined in a general equilibrium context and the results of the two policies not only on the environment, but also on the rest of the economy, can be compared. The advantage of CGE models over other empirical models is that they can capture the numerous complex relationships between variables in the model economy. Furthermore, only a general equilibrium evaluation of these policies can assess the impacts of their respective effects on welfare.

Outline of the Study

The existing literature on trade and the environment is surveyed in Chapter 2. This survey serves several purposes. Firstly, it identifies the reasons why trade can influence the environment. A summary of the interactions between trade and environmental policies and their efficiency, both at the national and international level, is presented. The political economy of policy instruments is also surveyed and evidence presented. Secondly, a description of how international trade can affect the environment is given. This is broken down into the three major effects, with evidence on environmental policy and competitiveness, as well as the pollution haven hypothesis being shown. Thirdly, the effects of trade liberalisation on the environment are discussed with reference to four major effects, and evidence presented. Lastly, the existing literature on CGE analyses of trade liberalisation's effects on the environment is examined.

Chapter 3 introduces the trade and environment issues in New Zealand. The geography and economy of New Zealand are described and some limited evidence on trade and environment in New Zealand is presented. New

Zealand's trade and environment policies are then detailed with the emphasis on trade liberalisation and the carbon dioxide emissions policy.

Chapter 4 is devoted to the description of the trade- and environment-focused multisectoral CGE model of New Zealand. The theoretical structure of the model is introduced and the policy simulations detailed. Special attention is paid to the treatment of imports and exports in international trade, as well as the environment. This is followed by a complete description of all the model equations.

In Chapter 5 the results of the policy simulation experiments performed using the multisectoral CGE model are presented. The effects of these policy simulations on the overall economy, emissions and welfare are detailed. It concludes with an interpretation of the results of the policy simulations.

In the final chapter, a summary of the major conclusions is presented, together with a brief discussion of the limitations of the exercise and some directions for future research.

— Chapter 2 —

Trade Liberalisation and the Environment: Theoretical Issues and Empirical Evidence

Introduction

This chapter presents a survey of the existing literature on the debate between trade and the environment and aims to examine the empirical evidence relating to the effects of trade liberalisation on the environment. This survey serves several purposes. First, it identifies the reasons why trade can influence the environment. A summary of the interactions between trade and environmental policies and their efficiency, both at the national and international level, is detailed. The political economy of policy instruments is also surveyed and evidence presented. Second, an analysis of how international trade can affect the environment is given. This is broken down into the three major effects namely the product, scale and structural effects. Third, the effects of trade liberalisation on the environment are discussed with reference to three major effects detailed above as well as a further effect, the regulatory effect, and evidence presented. Lastly, the existing literature on CGE analyses of trade liberalisation on the environment is examined.

Trade and Environmental Policy Links

Why international trade can affect the environment

Generally, market and intervention failures, rather than trade are the causes of environmental problems. Market failures occur where externalities exist, i.e. when markets do not reflect environmental values. Intervention failures occur when public policies do not correct for, create, or exacerbate market failures (OECD, 1994a). These failures can distort the economic agents' incentives for protecting the environment and can lead to a divergence between the private and socially optimal rates and composition of production and consumption. Understanding and correcting these failures at the domestic level have been the subject of environmental economics. However, these failures can also occur at the international level with significant effects. International trade can help correct market and intervention failures by providing increasing funds and incentives for environmental protection, and by promoting efficient resource use. However, international trade, may in some cases, exacerbate environmental problems in the presence of market and intervention failures.

Market failures

Market failures are due to the failure of markets to correctly value and allocate environmental assets. This means that the market prices of goods and services do not fully incorporate their environmental costs.

Externalisation of environmental costs

Market failures can result from the failure of polluters to take into account the environmental costs of their activities, so that the environmental costs are externalised rather than internalised in the prices of goods and services. Environmental externalities arise from the consumption of products that impose costs on others that are not compensated for via markets. This divergence of the internalised costs of an activity from its total cost may be reflected in the form of environmental degradation. Failure to internalise environmental costs at the national level can also contribute to transboundary and global environmental problems.

Improper valuation of ecosystems

Market failures also result from the failure to take into account the total economic value derived by society from the physical features and environmental functions of ecosystems.[1] The total economic value of the environment is categorised by OECD (1994a) into four different components, namely direct use values, indirect use values, existence values and option values. The direct use value of an environmental asset is the easiest to quantify and relates to the actual output of goods and services from the asset. While the benefits and costs of environmentally related services are harder to quantify than those of environmentally related goods, they are often more significant. The indirect use value of an environmental asset relates to its functional role in supporting economic activity, and is best measured in terms of the benefits derived from its contribution to the avoidance of environmental damage (e.g. protecting endangered species can indirectly maintain biodiversity, the loss of which might inhibit the further evolutionary capacity of all species). The existence value, relating to the benefits derived from the knowledge that an environmental asset exists and plays a functional role in maintaining ecosystems, as well as option values, associated with the future use of a resource (e.g. closed tropical forests which maintain biodiversity essential for future pharmaceutical research have an option value) have also been identified.

Poorly-defined property rights

Market failures can arise due to the lack of property rights for environmental assets and the difficulties of defining and enforcing these rights. The

[1]It should be noted that environmental values will differ across countries. Furthermore, only advanced countries presently have the institutional structures to decide on appropriate environmental policies. These structures are absent from developing countries and at the international level.

non-exclusive nature of environmental goods like air or water may lead to over-exploitation or over-consumption of a resource due to the lack of incentives to protect it against actions that would diminish its supply (e.g. lack of direct ownership of fisheries contributes to the depletion of world fish resources). Without the assignment or enforcement of property rights or some other form of government intervention, environmental assets are often susceptible to degradation. Furthermore, it may also lead to the failure to preserve them for future generations and thus their existence and option values may be eliminated.

Poorly-defined property rights can also play a role in global or transboundary environmental problems. Nations may make decisions regarding resource use that fail to take into account the costs and benefits to the world as a whole and to the global environment.

Intervention failures

It is difficult to separate the effects of different types of policies, including environmental policies, macroeconomic policies, microeconomic policies, or trade policies (OECD, 1994a). Most environmental problems are related to environmental policy intervention failures or the lack of appropriate environmental policies. Much analysis has been aimed at understanding, developing, and implementing domestic environment policies. However, far less is known about the environmental effects of other types of policies, such as trade policies, and how environmental considerations may be integrated into international markets.

Production and export subsidies, and trade barriers, can potentially worsen market failures and environmental policy failures by distorting resource values, input costs, and market prices for environmental goods and services (OECD, 1994a). This is especially true when governments create incentives through production and export subsidies which promote actions with adverse environmental effects, and when governments erect trade barriers which block market access and contribute to environmental problems in importing and exporting countries. Trade liberalisation initiatives are aimed at correcting these policy intervention failures and should have both trade and environmental benefits.

Subsidies

While most production subsidies are aimed at achieving domestic policy goals, they can also have implications for both trade and the environment, export subsidies have more direct impacts on trade flows and may also have environmental effects.

These effects are believed to be greatest in the agriculture sector (see OECD, 1994a). Subsidy policies, which in many countries influence the prices received by farmers and the cost of the inputs they use, can in fact augment rather than reduce market failures. In developed countries, output prices may be supported above market clearing levels and in some cases input prices are maintained below these levels. These policies can distort the response of agriculture producers to market signals and prevent the efficient use and allocation of resources. Production-related subsidies can promote more intensive agricultural production, thereby often exacerbating environmental problems related to the excessive use of chemicals, land or water use.

Trade barriers

Barriers to trade, such as tariffs, quotas and voluntary export restraints, may also constitute policy intervention failures, which accentuate existing market failures and the intervention failures of environmental policies. Trade protectionism can lead to trade distortions and prevent the efficient and environmentally beneficial allocation and use of resources. Support prices higher than world market levels often require, and are accompanied by, import barriers that distort the patterns of trade among countries and restrict market access for developing countries that are able to produce at lower cost. Having higher tariffs on processed goods compared to unprocessed goods (tariff escalation) can discourage the processing of primary commodities in producing countries and can contribute to the excessive exploitation of natural resources when exporters maximise their foreign exchange receipts.

Efficiency of policy instruments

In an open economy where production or consumption generates an externality such as pollution, there are various policies that can be used to achieve pollution abatement, such as emissions taxes, output taxes, or export taxes. In order to minimise the cost of pollution reduction, the optimal response would be the one most directly linked to the source of the externality. As such, trade policy responses are inferior to Pigouvian effluent taxes, abatement subsidies, or the assignment of property rights. Non-targeted instruments such as trade policy induce large welfare losses by distorting resource allocation beyond the source of the externality. This instrument assignment principle recognises the existence of different pollution abatement costs across polluters. For example, addressing a production externality with an output tax which is the same for all polluters is inefficient because it contracts output for all producers independent of their pollution levels (Beghin, Roland-Holst & van der Mensbrugghe, 1994a). Tariffs are even more inefficient than output taxes in this case, as they would penalise consumers of the commodity despite consumption having no bearing on the level of pollution. The optimal policy in these circumstances would be a targeted uniform tax per unit of pollution, as this would directly discourage pollutive emissions.

These clear-cut principles do not necessarily hold when some instruments are non-existent, difficult to implement, or require the employment of scarce institutional capacity (Bohm & Russell, 1985). It has been shown that in a second-best world trade policy, alone or in conjunction with environmental taxes, can be welfare improving. Copeland (1994) has shown this for small open economies with domestic pollution, Copeland (1991) for waste trade with some illegal disposal, Krutilla (1991) for large country cases, and Vasavada *et al.* (1993) for restrictions on available instruments. However, it must be noted that these studies involve narrow assumptions and as such cannot be generalised for practical use.

Economists still maintain the position that trade instruments should not be used to reduce pollution, even in a second-best world. Lloyd (1992) recognises the overall acceptance of the polluter pays principle (PPP) as evidence supporting direct (first-best) instruments in the real (second-best) world. The recent and continued move from command and control measures to market-based instruments in OECD countries is further evidence of the acceptance of these principles (OECD, 1993). The case against indirect instruments has been maintained by several empirical studies in second best settings, e.g. Lee & Roland-Holst (1994), Braga (1992) and Perroni & Wigle (1992). Since trade policy instruments do not usually have a direct or large impact on the pollution source, trade and resource allocation are significantly distorted by tariff-based environmental policies.

The direct policies and internalisation principles, supported by empirical research in developed countries, should be carefully applied in less developed countries. In these countries, trade policy instruments induce more rent-seeking activities than do other policies, this can have important income transfer effects dependent upon property rights to natural resources (Bell, 1990; Binswanger *et al.*, 1993; Taylor, 1993). Furthermore, institutional capacity may be well below that found in industrialised countries, monitoring, consistency, and enforcement of property rights and policies can be seriously deficient.[2] As a result, non-protectionist measures are preferable, and externalities are best addressed with incentive-based systems that minimise the costs and the levels of enforcement and infrastructure required.

There are, however, several empirical studies which show that the targeting principles from the developed countries are still applicable in less developed countries (i.e. tariffs and other trade policies are inferior instruments for achieving domestic environmental objectives). Lee & Roland-Holst (1994) show that tariffs are an inferior instrument in the control of pollution in Indonesia. Braga (1992), Gillis (1988a, b) and Barbier (1994) investigate the link between timber trade policy and environmental degradation in Indonesia, Brazil, Malaysia, Ghana and Liberia. Overall, they find that export bans are inferior in the internalisation of forest-related environmental problems, since they lower the domestic price for timber and increase domestic consumption. This conclusion was also reached for the United States in earlier studies.[3] The case for more direct policies such as royalties

[2]See Bell (1990), Binswanger *et al.* (1993) and Deacon (1992).

[3]See Sedjo & Wiseman (1983) and Parks & Cox (1985).

is less obvious. For forestry, Boado (1988) and Gillis (1988a, c) postulate that royalties increase deforestation by inducing "high-grading", which increases both waste and the areas disturbed.

Transboundary pollution and international policies

When the pollution source is outside national boundaries, do these targeting principles still apply? In the absence of international co-operation, it may be optimal for a single country to use trade policy measures in an attempt to reduce foreign environmental degradation. For example, Markusen (1975a, b) shows, in the absence of international co-operation, trade taxes can lower the price of the polluting good and internalise some of the associated welfare costs. Copeland (1993) looks at the case where transboundary pollution is internalised using a combined import tariff and process standard. However, these are shown to have the same results as would a tax on the pollution content of the imported good. These arguments do however rely on some specific assumptions including no retaliation.

International co-operation is the most efficient way to address transboundary environmental problems (Beghin, Roland-Holst & van der Mensbrugghe, 1994a). Policies can then be designed as for one country, for example equating marginal abatement costs across countries by using a per unit emissions charge. The importance of internationally co-ordinated policies to reduce carbon dioxide can be seen in Burniaux *et al.* (1992), Dean & Hoeller (1992), Martin *et al.* (1992) and Nordhaus (1991a, b), and it also led to the Montreal agreement on chlorofluorocarbons (CFCs) and halon reduction in 1990.

Unlike the case of producer pollution, there seem to be strong arguments for harmonisation of product standards to avoid protectionism. Furthermore, the only case where different standards appear to be economically legitimate are those in which the marginal benefits of incrementally more stringent standards exceed the costs of such standards (Dean, 1992).

It is the differences in absorptive capacity and social preferences that allows the environment to be treated as an endowment, or factor of production, that represents part of a country's comparative advantage, it follows that environmental standards and pollution abatement will be different among countries and there is no valid presumption in favour of uniformity of harmonisation (Low, 1992b).

One of the problems with international agreements is that not all countries have the same incentives to join, they are also characterised by free riding and monitoring problems. Martin *et al.* (1992) showed China and India would incur most of the cost of a uniform carbon tax and as such have little incentive to join. This can be reduced to some degree by transfers and international trade in emissions permits (Newbery, 1990; Maler, 1990; Bohm, 1992, 1993). But despite this, free riding and defection will always exist.

The threat of trade sanctions can be used to discourage free riding and enforce co-operation. For example, the Montreal agreement contains a clause which permits trade sanctions against non-complying countries. It is however, doubtful whether trade sanctions are an efficient means of reaching this objective. A more effective means may be to provide incentives to co-operate, such as the transfers available under the Montreal agreement, which introduces a cost of non-compliance. However, care should be taken so that these subsidies do not distort resource allocation and lead to increased environmental problems.

There are two main issues which link transnational pollution to trade and therefore to GATT. Are trade barriers an efficient way of reducing transnational pollution and if so, in what way must the GATT rules be modified to allow for this? Secondly, how will domestic environmental regulations controlling transnational pollution affect the pattern of trade? Baumol & Oates (1988) address the theoretical question of the optimal policy response to transnational externalities. They argue that an internationally optimal tax on emissions is required, one that is equal to the marginal damage generated in all countries taken together. However, given national sovereignty, this would be very difficult to implement. They conclude, given their analysis, that no tariff can sustain the Pareto-optimum which is the result of the optimal tax. They also argue that there is a "quasi-optimal" tariff as a second-best policy, and conclude that although tariffs are clearly second-best, there may be a role for them to move the global economy in the direction of a "quasi-optimum", or alternatively as a threat to enforce compliance with an internationally agreed target. Merrifield (1989), Whalley (1991) and Whalley & Wigle (1991) have also performed further work in this field.

Diwan & Shafik (1992) demonstrated that, in a situation of less than perfectly functioning markets for capital and emissions, the liberalisation of one market and not the other may lead to a harmful environmental outcome. The only mechanism (from cash transfers, debt for nature swaps, technology transfers, and sanctions for nature) that does not have negative side effects, is the transfer of clean or pollution-reducing technology, and the negative effects of the others can be significant. Sadafi & Low (1992) use a game-theoretic model to see what types of co-operation are efficient in terms of environmental outcomes as a binding agreement. However their model assumes threats are credible, and so international agreements may be elusive. Furthermore, the search for international agreements may distract attention away from domestic environmental policy and result in the environment being worse off. Robertson (1992a) views the desire for an international agreement as merely a means of avoiding domestic environmental issues. Sorsa (1992) looks at the GATT, and concludes that since trade is seldom the source of environmental problems, there is little sense in its use in addressing these problems. The GATT poses little threat to the legitimate pursuit of environmental objectives. Where they do intersect there is usually a means of addressing the problem. At most, the GATT may require some clarification in a few areas like border adjustments, and the relation between GATT and other international agreements containing trade provisions. A superior alternative would be to use separate environmental agreements rather than the GATT to solve environmental problems.

Generally, it is reasonable to argue that the GATT is in more need of protection from poorly reasoned demands for reform based on environmental arguments, than the environment is from the rules of the international trading system (Low, 1992b).

Political economy of policy instruments

Given the recognition by economists that trade policies are generally inadequate instruments for addressing environmental externalities, the prevalence for their use in environmental ends is puzzling (Beghin, Roland-Holst & van der Mensbrugghe, 1994). This situation arises mainly from the political economy of rent-seeking. Rent-seeking interest groups pressure policy makers to adopt policies that benefit them, but which are inefficient for the economy as a whole. This occurs because they view the welfare losses as small compared to the expected environmental gains (Hillman & Ursprung, 1992). Other interest groups may also favour trade restrictions for other protectionist reasons and this can in turn result in coalitions between environmental and industrial lobby groups. Environmentalists tend to view trade policy as a means of raising domestic environmental standards and inducing countries to join and abide by international environmental agreements. Environmentalists also believe that by joining protectionist groups facing declining competitiveness due to high domestic environmental standards, they can give incentives for foreign firms to raise standards (Drake-Brockman & Anderson, 1994).

Hoekman & Leidy (1992) discuss how quantitative regulations like product and process standards can influence the trade and environment link through trade flow distortions and rent-seeking interest groups. Fixed production factors prefer output regulation to pollution taxes since factor rewards may not be as affected. Standards can also be manipulated so as to restrict entry into the industry as well. Quantity regulation also tends to favour collusive behaviour. Environmentalists tend to be process-oriented as this imposes cleaner technology on firms and because they prefer the maximum abatement possible. Product standards can also be manipulated to protect domestic producers from foreign competition. Process standards may result in import bans as domestic groups pressure for "fair" trade. When standards relate to the production process and not the product, all imports may be restricted instead of just environmentally unfriendly ones, which contravenes GATT rules. A popular example of this is the United States ban on Mexican Tuna because some Mexican Tuna was caught using methods damaging to dolphins. As there was no way of telling by the final product what catching method was employed, all imports of Mexican Tuna were banned. However, the GATT Dispute Panel ruled this ban inconsistent with international trading rules. Similarly, restrictions on unrelated products are also GATT inconsistent, for example restricting textile imports to stop tropical timber logging. Hahn (1990) also provides a good summary of the literature on the political economy of environmental policies.

Subramanian (1992) and Blackhurst & Subramanian (1992) give a useful taxonomy of trade policies for environmental objectives and differentiate between those policies used as protectionism and the GATT-legitimate uses of trade policy measures. The GATT allows only a few cases of lawful trade policy interventions to address environmental problems, using the following criteria: non-discrimination, non-protectionism, national treatment, necessity or minimum trade restrictiveness and scope.[4] The OECD guidelines on environmental policies follow the same philosophy of minimising trade distortions, and accentuating national treatment, non-discrimination and transparency. However, the actual policy menu adopted by OECD members is diverse and often follows a regulatory approach (Barde, 1994).

With respect to the issue of international standards harmonisation, GATT has been trying to foster the adoption of minimum non-protectionist standards as a way to circumvent unilateral manipulation of these standards for protectionist aims (Beghin, Roland-Holst & van der Mensbrugghe, 1994a). The OECD is following the same pragmatic strategy with its guidelines on harmonisation (OECD, 1994a).

New environmental regulation instruments are being developed such as environmental packaging, eco-labelling and recycling requirements in order to encourage life cycle management of products. Even though these policies are preferable to less direct trade policies, the potential remains for these policies to result in protectionist outcomes. Eco-labelling which provides information that is potentially valuable to consumers is an example of standards that affect the characteristics of the final product. As such, the market prices should reflect the differences in their environmental characteristics. Some of these standards like eco-packaging may not be consistent with Article XI of GATT, which prohibits such restrictions. However it should be noted that due to substitution effects, labelling can have the negative effect of lowering the price of the environmentally unfriendly goods and thus increasing their consumption. Also, if eco-standards are made

[4]See OECD (1994b), Sorsa (1992) and Lloyd (1992).

compulsory and affect trade, they are increasingly likely to be manipulated in favour of protectionism.

Van Grasstek (1992), for the United States, and Klepper (1992), for Germany, provide some limited evidence of collusion between environmental groups and sectoral interest groups for protection. Van Grasstek (1992) investigates voting behaviour of United States legislators to identify manipulation of trade for environmental objectives. The overlapping interests of domestic industries and environmentalists in the United States appear to be limited. Environmental protectionism does however occur in the financing of environmental policies which discriminate against imports or impose process standards on imported goods, or which impose trade sanctions for violation of environmental safeguards. There is some indication of legislators enacting "green" protectionist policies when their own state depends on dirty industries. They appeal to consumers and protect their state's producers, thereby reaping a double dividend politically.

Klepper (1992) does not find such a problem of environmentalists and protectionists co-operating together in the European Community (EC) because environmental policy is domestic whereas trade policy is determined by the EC as a whole. However, the issue of environmental standards has given rise to intense debate and lobbying in the EC.

How International Trade Can Affect the Environment

Depending on the circumstances, international trade flows can have both positive and negative effects on the environment. Those most commonly identified in the literature are product (or technology) effects, related to the commercial exchange of goods and services, scale effects, related to the expansion of markets and economic activity, and structural effects, related to the distribution and intensity of production and consumption activities.

Product effects

In terms of positive product effects, trade can have significant positive effects on environmental quality as the mechanism by which goods, which contribute to environmental protection and substitutes for environmentally damaging products, are diffused. Trade also provides the opportunity for the international exchange of environmental technologies and services to address specific environmental problems. The market for environmental equipment and services, which include products for water and effluent treatment, waste management, air quality control, land remediation and noise abatement, is now estimated at US$200 billion worldwide and growing at a rate of 5.5 per cent per year (OECD, 1994a). Trade has the effect of expanding markets for goods produced by environmentally beneficial production methods and promotes the international exchange of environmentally sound inputs, thereby raising the levels of environmental protection both in producing and consuming countries. Improvements in production technology can reduce all inputs in proportion to one another (unbiased technological change), or it can reduce the use of one input relative to another (biased technological change). In either case, if technological change improves the efficiency with which environmental inputs can be used, it will reduce the environmental intensity of production (Globerman, 1993).

In the absence of optimal environmental policies trade can have negative product effects through the international exchange of goods that directly harm the environment, such as hazardous wastes, dangerous chemicals and endangered species. Certain wastes and chemicals which are harmful to man and the environment through their explosive, toxic, corrosive, or carcinogenic characteristics are transported and traded internationally and are currently the subject of trade controls (OECD, 1994a). Other products in international trade may also be damaging through more indirect environmental impacts, such as chemical residues on agriculture products, or packaging that is not biodegradable or recyclable.

Scale effects

Some of the environmental effects of trade are a result of trade increasing the overall level or scale of economic activity and growth. Trade can have a positive scale effect by raising incomes so that there is a greater demand for, and more funds available to spend on, environmental protection. Trade increases the efficiency of international markets through the free flow of goods and services, which enables resources to be allocated in production according to the principles of least cost and highest return. Hence, trade allows countries with different resource endowments and comparative advantages to free themselves from constraints to growth due to their domestic limits. Trade-driven economic growth provides countries both with the financial resources to deal with environmental problems, and raises national environmental preferences through per capita income growth.

However, trade-induced growth, which occurs in the presence of market and intervention failures, may have certain negative scale effects, making it less sustainable in the long run. Greater economic activity raises demand for all goods, hence increases emissions as well as the use of environmental inputs. Trade may aggravate environmental problems when the expansion of global economic activities occurs in the absence of measures to control the possible detrimental environmental impacts that are caused by market and intervention failures. The market expansion and growth resulting from trade may lead to increased degradation and more rapid depletion of scarce natural resources due to continuing failures to internalise environmental costs, to correctly value the environment, and to define, assign, and enforce property rights. Therefore, trade's positive contributions for the environment are realised in the presence of socially optimal environmental policies.

Structural effects

The structural effects of trade, which are more indirect than product or scale effects, relate to the composition of production and resource use deriving from trade-related factors. In this case, the role of trade is difficult to separate from many other contributing variables. However it is believed that trade may have an impact on the environment by altering the international location and intensity of production and consumption activities via its effect on market prices. Trade, by maximising allocative efficiency among countries, can have positive structural effects in allocating economic activity in accordance with countries environmental endowments and conditions, as well as promoting the efficient use of resources. If environmental assets are correctly valued and measured, their value taken into account in international prices and markets, their use not distorted by government policy interventions, trade would be the ideal vehicle for furthering sustainable development at the global level (OECD, 1994a).

In the absence of the ideal case, trade may alternatively have negative structural effects by locating production and consumption in geographic areas that are unsuited to the nature or intensity of the activity. Due to market and intervention failures (most common of which are the environmental policy failures), trade can contribute to patterns of production, which do not reflect the environmental endowments of countries. In some countries, natural resources may remain under utilised, whereas in others, production activities may exceed levels the environment can accommodate. In certain cases, trade may lead to production patterns that are based on large-scale inputs such as chemicals, energy or capital, rather than on the sustainable use of natural endowments.

However, trade flows are generally not the causal factor, structural effects on the environment have a small effect relative to market and policy intervention failures. Most often, the structural effects of trade in sectors such as industry and transport arise primarily from the failure to internalise environmental costs in the prices of goods and services.

Environmental policy and competitiveness

Environmental policies can affect firms' production costs and therefore also affect trade patterns. Two prevailing views exist on the relationship between environmental regulations and international competitiveness. The first maintains that stringent environmental regulations impose significant costs on domestic firms and industries, thus reducing their international competitiveness compared to those with less stringent environmental regulations.[5] The opposite view is attributable to Porter (1991) and Porter & Linde (1995) who

[5]This loss of competitiveness is claimed to be greater in "pollution-intensive" industries, defined in the literature as those products with direct and indirect pollution abatement costs constituting at least 1.85 per cent of total production costs in the United States (see Low & Yeats (1992) for details).

claim that more stringent environmental regulations lead to productivity improvements because of a cleaner environment and the stimulating effect of regulations on innovations. In addition, those countries that impose stringent environmental regulations earlier, and invest in cleaner technology would be able to create a comparative advantage in environmentally sensitive industries.[6] Compliance with higher environmental regulations could also be an additional source of structural adjustment in particular for developing economies as these regulations will promote less pollution-intensive industries (Sorsa, 1994). While environmental degradation is not internalised in production costs resource allocation will be inefficient. In an open economy this means a non-optimal pattern of trade. The early theoretical work on competitiveness and the environment looked at the effects of environmental policies on comparative advantage and trade in simple trade models. In these (surveyed in Siebert, 1985), pollution is treated as a factor of production, and environmental policies (which reflect how societies value the environment) as well as the country's absorptive capacity, determine whether pollution is abundant or scarce. A country is thought to have an environmental abundance if it has a relatively large assimilative capacity (i.e. can tolerate more pollutants). Blackhurst (1977) describes assimilative capacity as being influenced by the physical ability of water, air and land, to absorb waste as well as the level of pollutants society is willing to tolerate. The standard result is that countries with a large absorptive capacity tend to have a comparative advantage in pollution-intensive activities. These models also predict that less developed countries will specialise in pollution-intensive production (Copeland & Taylor, 1993).

Looking at the theoretical literature, there appears to be justification for concern that countries with more stringent environmental regulations could suffer a loss in comparative advantage in affected sectors. It is also clear that some re-allocation of resources from the pollution-intensive sector is desirable, to the extent that the present allocation does not accurately reflect assimilative capacities.

[6]This view has been criticised by Oates *et al.* (1993) and Palmer *et al.* (1995).

Since perceptions about the existence and degree of externalities are unlikely to be the same among countries, this leads to the conclusion that the imposition of a pollution abatement equalisation tax, or any similar attempt to "level the playing field" would be strongly suggestive of protectionism, with little or no environmental justification (Low, 1992b). Trade barriers are an inefficient and costly means for one country to attempt to induce another to internalise environmental externalities, and far from guarantee a positive environmental result. International co-operation on the environment, on the other hand, is much more likely to have the desired results. The protectionism likely to result from internationally uniform environmental policies is revealed by the fact that these policies aim to equate pollution abatement costs rather than to achieve equality of environmental standards, irrespective of differences in costs of abatement. Harmonisation of standards permits direct control of environmental policy internationally, and allows the imposition of external preferences, however differing absorptive capacities and social discount rates provide strong grounds for reservations about uniformity as an international environmental policy objective (Low, 1992b).

Some policy measures have been implemented in the OECD in response to loss of competitiveness. Examples of these are subsidies to meet environmental standards, and countervailing duties to maintain competitiveness, however, these policies should not be allowed by GATT. Furthermore, taxes or marketable permits are more efficient means of meeting environmental objectives (Dean, 1992).

Despite this, studies do not find strong evidence that environmental regulations specifically have had any affect on competitiveness. Overall, the effect of environmental regulations on commodity prices seems to be minimal. OECD (1993), Tobey (1990) and Walter (1973), estimate abatement costs at between one and three per cent of total production costs. Low (1992b) finds that environmental control costs (ECC) are small, weighted average equal to only 0.54 per cent in 1988, with the highest ratio for cement being only just over three per cent. This difference between low environmental control costs and less developed countries specialisation in pollution-intensive goods may be due to a measurement problem, or because abatement costs do not fully capture all the costs of environmental regulations.

Robertson (1992a) deals with these issues in greater depth, as does Sorsa (1992). Robertson emphasises the costs of international harmonisation of standards relating to the suppression of social choice and elimination of competition. It is also important to distinguish between product and process standards. Product standards (externalities in consumption) should be enforced in a certain location irrespective of the source. Process standards (externalities in production) should be location-specific and standards harmonisation should be seen as protectionist. If the process involves international externalities, then concern over process standards may be legitimate, however this does not mean there is a case for standards harmonisation as long as social preferences between countries differ. The most efficient way for countries to induce others into higher standards is to provide them with incentives to do so (Diwan & Shafik, 1992).

Not all arguments oppose harmonisation. Differentiated standards may increase the transaction costs of trade, as well as production costs. They may also serve as a protectionist mechanism. Environment and competitiveness issues are basically about the avoidance of protectionism via environmental arguments. The competitive disadvantage resulting from differences in environmental policies may not be great (either due to differing standards or differing enforcement), however more research is required to reach an immutable conclusion. Even if pollution abatement costs were significant this would still not be justification for measures aimed at equalising costs, nor the harmonisation of standards.

Several studies have analysed the theoretical impact of environmental policy on standard results in trade — Siebert (1977, 1985), Pethig (1976), McGuire (1982), Baumol & Oates (1988) and Blackhurst (1977). Siebert (1985) summarises many of these studies regarding the impact of environmental policy on comparative advantage. By assuming countries have identical production, pollution and abatement functions for a particular good, then under free trade it would be expected that the country with the relatively larger assimilative capacity would specialise in the relatively more pollution-intensive good. It is assumed that the country with the largest endowment of assimilative capacity will have a price advantage in the pollution-intensive good. However when pollution costs are not fully internalised, then this price advantage will be magnified and as such excessive specialisation of this good occurs.

With the unilateral imposition of environmental regulations by the environmentally rich country, it will impose environmental control costs on its producers, thus eroding their price advantage relative to foreign countries, this will reduce the location disadvantage of the environmentally scarce country. Therefore a shift in specialisation can be expected, where the environmentally scarce country increases its production of the pollution-intensive good. Unilateral regulations therefore alter the pattern of trade and increase pollution in the environmentally scarce country, even when no transnational pollution exists. If both countries were then to adopt optimal environmental regulation, so that production internalised all costs of pollution, then it can be expected world output of the pollution-intensive good would fall. However, it can also be expected that the environmentally rich country would retain its comparative advantage in the pollution-intensive good. Optimal regulation of pollution should change the pattern of trade to reflect the relative assimilative capacities of the trading partners. However, it is unclear whether unilateral regulations will move the pattern of trade closer to the optimum or not (Dean, 1992).

There are a number of studies that have attempted to estimate the impact of ECC on industry price and output, and on the pattern of trade. (D'Arge, 1974; OECD, 1978; Magee & Ford, 1972; Pasurka, 1985; Richardson & Mutti, 1976, 1977; Walter, 1973; Ugelow, 1982; US DOC, 1975; Robinson, 1988; Tobey, 1990.) The methodologies employed are quite varied so comparison of these studies is difficult, however some generalisations can be made. Estimates of ECC by industry tend to be very low, abatement costs constitute only a small portion of total industry costs on average. Reductions in output caused by ECC also tend to be small and insignificant on average, although they can be significant for some selected sectors. Also, there is little evidence of any significant impact of ECC on the pattern of trade.

Lucas, Wheeler & Hettige (1992) and Low & Yeats (1992), both empirically address the issue of pollution-intensive industry migration. Lucas *et al.* look at the relationship between income levels and pollution intensities, and between trade policy and pollution. Industrial pollution levels depend both on the size of the industrial base and the pollution intensity of the industries involved. Sectoral composition is only one of the factors influencing pollution intensity, other factors are technology choice, pollution abatement activity, and productive efficiency. Pollution-intensive industries have located in less developed countries, but the question is whether they have migrated. There is no evidence that industries have uprooted from industrial countries (Low, 1992b). Low & Yeats find that there has been a disproportionately large increase in the number of developing countries with revealed comparative advantages (RCAs) in most of the polluting industries. The rate at which developing countries acquired RCAs in dirty industries in the period examined (1965–1988) was four times as great as that of industrial countries and faster than the average for all industries in less developed countries. However, it is not conclusive as to why this happened and may only be dispersion rather than displacement. It could also be due to labour costs or natural resource endowments, or because particularly pollutive industries dominate the early stages of development. If ECC rises significantly in the future, then environmental policy regimes may become an important factor in the location decisions of firms. Some statistics are suggestive of the use of relatively more pollutive technologies in less developed countries in terms of carbon dioxide emissions, but this may be merely a difference in industry composition.

Pollution haven and industrial flight hypotheses

Another concern of having lower environmental standards in developing countries compared with those in industrialised countries is that it will lead to pollution-intensive industries relocating their operations to these less developed countries (the industrial flight hypothesis). Less developed countries may also purposely undervalue the environment in order to attract new investment (the pollution haven hypothesis). Both these events could lead to an inefficient (excessive) level of pollution in less developed countries. As noted above, some relocation of pollution-intensive goods production is optimal since countries possess different assimilative capacities, however Pearson (1987) notes there is no reason to believe that less developed countries are relatively more environmentally abundant than developed countries.

Empirical studies tend to corroborate developing economies specialising in pollution-intensive industries as well as the global capacity and output of pollution-intensive industries shifting to less developed countries. Hettige, Lucas & Wheeler (1992) and Lucas, Wheeler & Hettige (1992) find that pollution intensity is greater in low income countries, which is consistent with specialisation in pollution-intensive activities where absorptive capacity is economically abundant. Birdsall & Wheeler (1992), Low & Yeats (1992) and OECD (1993) also have similar findings. Other studies focusing on the pollution intensity of trade between developed and less developed countries,* also find that the less developed countries export relatively pollutive products and developed countries export relatively less pollutive products.

The fact that the observed difference between low environmental control costs, and less developed countries specialisation in pollution-intensive goods described above, may be due to measurement problems or because abatement costs do not fully capture all the costs of environmental regulations. This could also be the reason why studies do not support the pollution haven hypothesis. This lack of evidence as recorded by Leonard (1988) is not unexpected given the difficult task of estimating how regulations influence investment decisions (Lucas, 1993). It could also be due to weak environmental regulations accompanying political instability, future uncertainty concerning regulation or corruption. It may be the case that these costs nullify all benefits from lower environmental standards.

How International Trade Liberalisation Can Affect the Environment

Similar to trade flows, trade liberalisation may have both positive and negative environmental impacts. The impacts of trade liberalisation result

*For example, between Japan and Indonesia (see Lee & Roland-Holst, 1994).

from its obvious purpose, which is to change existing trade policies in the direction of freer trade. Because of this, trade can have significant positive impacts on the environment by correcting existing trade policy intervention failures. It may also have some negative impacts related to an expansion of trade in the absence of correcting other existing market and policy intervention failures. In addition to the product, scale and structural effects described above for trade flows, OECD (1994a) identifies a further category of effects trade liberalisation may have, namely regulatory effects, in its implications for environmental standards and policies.

Product effects

The product effects of trade liberalisation are determined by how the removal of barriers to trade change the product composition of trade. Positive product effects deriving from increased trade and the transfer of environmental technologies and services will help offset the potential negative scale and structural effects arising from freer trade. Removal of import and export controls, improved intellectual property right systems, and other trade liberalising steps should promote the international exchange and dissemination of environmentally clean techniques and commodities. Increased trade can also benefit the environment by facilitating greater access to less environmentally harmful inputs, for example low sulphur coal instead of high sulphur coal, and recyclable inputs. Technological developments can permanently alter the structure of inputs in consumption and production activities. Free trade can also be expected to accelerate the rate of adoption of new technology, however it is not obvious that this technological change will be biased towards or away from the use of environmental inputs.

Freer trade may also require increased attention and monitoring of trade in environmentally hazardous or sensitive goods. For example, trade liberalisation could facilitate the international movement of toxic wastes, hazardous chemicals and endangered species, and demand enhanced co-operative efforts to avoid environmental accidents or potential environmental degradation.

Scale effects

Trade liberalisation should lead to positive scale effects by accelerating growth and increasing the financial resources that can be used to address environmental problems. In general, it is easier to raise levels of environmental protection in a growing economy (OECD, 1994a). Trade-related growth can provide the resources for companies to invest in cleaner technologies and the government with revenues for financing environmental infrastructure such as sewage treatment and water supply. Trade liberalisation leads to higher income levels by encouraging increased efficiency in the allocation of resources. It follows that the demand for goods and services should increase with corresponding increases in consumption and production. The impact this has on the environment depends on the relative shifts in demand between products and relative shifts in production technologies arising from the different income elasticities of demand for the various products. New products may enter at higher income levels, and demand for environmentally harmful goods may fall. Increased competition associated with trade liberalisation should encourage improved technical efficiency as firms utilise optimally sized plants and specialise production within plants to realise economies of scale. Increased competition should stimulate a faster rate of adoption of the latest technology, including technology associated with the direct or indirect use of environmental inputs. Overall, this should lead to more efficient use of all inputs, including the environment.

However, there is also concern relating to potential negative scale effects, which may result from pollution associated with the expansion of economic activity as well as greater movement of tradeable goods. Increased specialisation could lead to increased intra-industry trade, which may imply a higher degree of cross border shipments of products. Since transportation tends to be relatively environmentally intensive, this is likely to increase the use of environmental inputs. However, total use of environmental inputs need not increase if this increase in transportation occurs in high environmental standard areas relative to low environmental standard areas. The environmental effects of trade liberalisation with regard to border pollution, overall air and water quality, and risks of accidents may not be completely compensated by the advantages that result from higher economic growth. Therefore, trade liberalisation should give consideration to environmental policies which can help guarantee the sustainability of this growth.

Structural effects

The main environmental benefits of trade liberalisation are due to the positive structural effects of removing trade-distorting policies. Trade liberalisation should reduce or dispense with many policy interventions that now intensify environmental problems through their distortive effects on the location and intensity of production and consumption. Freer trade through the removal of trade barriers should re-distribute world production with some countries increasing production and others reducing production of different goods. It should also encourage countries to specialise to a greater extent in sectors in which they enjoy a comparative advantage, including those advantages based on environmental endowments.

The possibility of negative structural effects from trade liberalisation derives from the expansion of trade in the presence of market and intervention failures, which could in certain cases, worsen the allocation and intensity of economic activities with respect to their effect on the environment. Increased production of certain goods and services following trade liberalisation could in the absence of optimal environmental policies but in the presence of market externalities, lead to intensified environmental degradation. Countries with lower environmental standards and enforcement may attract environmentally intensive activities that are increasingly uneconomical to carry out in higher standard countries following trade liberalisation. Furthermore, this may increase the demand for environmentally damaging production if this expansion in environmentally-intensive production in the low standard nation is at the expense of clean production techniques in the high standard nation, so that overall production is on average more environmentally harmful. It is the existence of market and intervention failures, that allows the negative structural effects of trade liberalisation to occur, where environmental values may not be fully internalised in the prices of traded goods and/or optimal environmental policies or sustainable management practices may not be present. Furthermore, trade liberalisation may not be complete or entirely encompassing and some distortive trade policy interventions may remain following the liberalisation initiatives.

Regulatory effects

In addition to the above types of effects, trade liberalisation may also have positive and negative regulatory effects, which relate to how trade policy changes impact on existing environmental policies and standards. Trade liberalisation agreements may affect environmental policies by promoting harmonisation of national policies, particularly environmental standards, in order to facilitate trade. National environmental subsidies, environment-related fiscal measures, and environment-related trade measures, may all be affected by trade liberalisation. Trade agreements may have connotations for the level and enforcement of environmental process standards by providing incentives to changes in investment and industry location. Trade liberalisation also has the potential to weaken or strengthen national trade-related commitments under international environmental agreements.

Overall trade liberalisation should assist in lifting overall levels of environmental protection as more attention and resources are directed at strengthening environmental laws and enforcement in countries where they may be less than satisfactory. There is widespread concern however that the regulatory effects of trade may not be totally positive.

Increased competition associated with trade liberalisation may lead producers to "cheat" on their environmental standards and/or lead to increased lobbying efforts to have environmental standards relaxed (Emerson & Mickesell, 1991). Alternatively national governments may be less inclined to pass and enforce environmental standards given industrial migration and short-term unemployment associated with adjustments to trade liberalisation. Another possibility is that governments will lower environmental standards to "level the playing field". However, the proposition that trade liberalisation leads to a *de facto* harmonisation of environmental standards at the "lowest common denominator" is not supported by the evidence in the United States and the EC. The EC experience is evidence of the difficulties of harmonising environmental standards across trading partners, however it also suggests that the harmonisation of standards will be in the direction of the most restrictive standards.

It is also argued that trade agreements should be used as a lever to extract higher environmental standards from other countries. However, it should be recognised that this has the potential for the social costs of environmental regulation to exceed the social benefits.

It has been established theoretically that it is rarely welfare improving to impose trade restrictions in response to being polluted by another country's producers or consumers (Lloyd, 1992). This result in addition to the recognition that lobby groups use environmental issues to extract import protection suggests that environmental problems should be treated separately from trade issues. In general, positive regulatory effects of trade liberalisation can be assured if governments are able to pursue effective environmental policies.

Relationship between trade liberalisation, growth and the environment

An important recent development in the literature has been the decomposition of pollution into three underlying components — attributable respectively to composition (structural), technology (product) and scale effects as described above (Grossman & Krueger, 1992; Copeland & Taylor, 1994). Copeland & Taylor (1994) investigate how economic growth affects the location of pollution-intensive industries. Growth with trade as opposed to autarky induces three main effects — a scale effect that always increases pollution, a composition (structural) effect and a technical (product) effect. In this decomposition, based on the empirical work of Grossman & Krueger (1992), it is assumed that the environment is a normal good, and higher income induces tougher environmental standards and the adoption of environmentally cleaner technology.

The synthesis of growth, trade and the environment is made more complex because scientific understanding of ecosystems is limited (Solow, 1991). The long-term relationship between effluents and economic development is neither well understood nor well documented (Hettige, Lucas &

Wheeler, 1992; Grossman & Krueger, 1992; World Bank, 1992). For example in high income countries, pollution related to solid waste, groundwater contamination and global warming is still increasing with economic growth. Grossman (1993) and World Bank (1992) show that not all effluent growth follows an inverted-U shape. Hettige, Lucas & Wheeler (1992) actually show that pollution intensities per unit of industrial output increase with economic development. The structural effect appears to be more important than the product effect in explaining lower pollution per unit of wealth created in developed countries. Pollution related to transport increases markedly with more specialisation, market integration and urbanisation (OECD, 1993). Furthermore, there is nothing automatic about the reduction of some pollutants with growth, implied by the inverted-U pattern found for some pollutants. An intricate synthesis of technical change, income effects and public pressure for a cleaner environment leads to lower pollution intensity of output because of cleaner technology and a change in the composition of output and consumption (O'Connor, 1994).

Trade promotes competition, which in turn leads to reduced waste and more efficient use of energy resources. Therefore, trade pressures may contribute to the decline of some pollutants induced by growth because of more efficient international specialisation. International competition and undistorted price signals increase allocative efficiency and decrease pollution through more economic pricing and use of energy resources (Lucas, Wheeler & Hettige, 1992; Ten Kate & Draaisma, 1994). This is a case of a "win-win" or "no regret" situation with a better environment and larger pie (World Bank, 1992).

In inward-oriented countries, the State often escaped competitive market discipline and political accountability, and was often itself the worst polluter and violator of environmental regulations within the economy (e.g. public enterprises in the Soviet countries, the Mexican oil sector, and the forest resources of many countries) (Beghin, Roland-Holst & van der Mensbrugghe, 1994a).

Unilateral trade liberalisation may not lead to overall welfare gains when pollution-intensive exports expand. At the same time, the welfare of the importing country can improve. This is an example of a welfare transfer induced by "pollution cost transfer" (Pethig, 1976; Asako, 1979). Copeland

(1994) looks at this issue and concludes that trade liberalisation, when accompanied by environmental policies internalising externalities, is beneficial.

One of the major arguments with respect to the environment, growth and trade linkage is that absorptive capacity changes with economic development and this in turn affects comparative advantage and consumption which both induce new trade patterns. Outward-oriented trade strategies promote the international division of labour, which may imply pollution-intensive goods specialisation at low levels of development, although the evidence suggests that specialisation occurred in both labour-intensive and pollution-intensive industries (Hettige, Lucas & Wheeler, 1992). International trade also facilitates the international transfer and adoption of cleaner technology and allows latecomers to do technological leapfrogging (Hettige, Lucas & Wheeler, 1992; O'Connor, 1994). A product effect can occur when specialisation and demands for a cleaner environment influence the location of production to where the technology is the most advanced and often cleanest. Cleaner technology then becomes more easily available in a global world, and is also more highly demanded since the environment is now more highly valued (Copeland & Taylor, 1994).

When externalities are properly internalised, growth will improve welfare, however pollution continues to increase (at a decreasing rate), and as such growth increases pollution. New technology is therefore the only way to break the growth pollution link. Lopez (1992) finds that if the environment is treated as a resource in future production then pollution can decrease with growth since the environment has an opportunity cost in future production.

Wheeler & Martin (1992) analyse international transfers of technology in the wood pulp industry, and show the positive effect of competition on the adoption of cleaner technologies.

During the Uruguay Round of the GATT, several papers investigated the environmental implications of multilateral trade liberalisation (Anderson, 1992b; Cook & Tobey, 1992; IFPRI, 1990; Lutz, 1992; OECD, 1994a; Runge, 1994). Actual empirical estimates are rare in the literature. Most papers have identified the likely environmental impacts for agricultural trade liberalisation but welfare estimates for quantified environmental impacts of reforms are non-existent. A common view has evolved that the environment in developed economies will benefit from a reduction in distortions in agriculture markets.

On the other hand, less developed economies would experience the opposite changes following GATT-induced trade liberalisation. There is likely to be an increase in the use of fertilisers and pesticides due to the higher output prices. The overall net effect on land (including improved property rights, land expansion and less poverty-driven deforestation) however is uncertain.

The impact of trade liberalisation on the environment may often be negative in the short term since use of natural resources (even when appropriately priced), increases with the expansion in output that accompanies the reform (Lee & Roland-Holst, 1994). In theory, increased pollution does not necessarily decrease welfare in the presence of optimal environmental policies. However, the general presumption is that optimal environmental policies are not in place, or may not be properly enforced in less developed countries. Grossman & Krueger (1992) show that under NAFTA, Mexico would actually specialise in unskilled labour-intensive activities, the United States would increase its output in pollution-intensive capital-intensive industries, whereas Mexico's most polluting industries would contract.

The trade and environment debate has evolved considerably over the years, first pressure to use trade instruments for environmental ends were discounted as an indirect and inefficient approach to environmental policy (Anderson & Blackhurst, 1992). Co-ordination of trade liberalisation with the introduction of targeted environmental policies is supported by theoretical analyses of trade and environmental linkages (Copeland, 1994; Beghin, Roland-Holst & van der Mensbrugghe, 1994b).

Radetski (1992) argues that increased levels of economic activity are associated with improved environmental conditions. The high income elasticity of demand for environmental quality, structural shifts towards cleaner environmental activities at higher income levels, and the extension of property rights combined with the development of policies to deal with global common externalities in more developed countries are identified as key factors in this relationship. Radetski also gives a variety of empirical evidence to support the contention that the pollution intensity of production and consumption falls as incomes rise (i.e. inverted-U relationship).

Lucas *et al.* (1992) test for existence of an inverted-U shaped relationship and find evidence of its existence. However, they also find that it does not hold for pollution intensity with respect to manufacturing output.

Diwan & Shafik (1992) point out that global carbon emissions continue to rise with incomes as increases in the capital stock have dominated improvements in the capital stock.

Discussion of growth and the environment is closely related to the discussion of trade liberalisation and the environment particularly due to the large body of evidence associating trade liberalisation with increased growth. It is therefore obvious that trade liberalisation can have both positive and negative effects on the environment. Lucas *et al.* (1992) and Birdsall & Wheeler (1992) both perform statistical tests on the relationship between the degree of trade openness, growth and environmental quality. Lucas *et al.* show that fast growing closed economies became significantly more pollution-intensive in the 1970s and 1980s, whereas the opposite was true for more open economies. Fast growing open economies experienced mainly pollution-neutral structural change in the 1970s and a significant shift towards a less pollution-intensive structure in the 1980s.

Birdsall & Wheeler present similar evidence to the above but with reference solely to Latin America. They also find similar trends to the global developing country data, where pollution-intensive industries have tended to locate in the less open economies. The choice of technology can be influenced by, fear of liability in relation to environmental accidents, desire to protect the firm's reputation, costs of unbundling technology, "green consumerism" in export markets, anticipation of future environmental regulation, and the high cost of retrofitting capital equipment (Lopez, 1992). If open economies attract more foreign investment then these technological factors are likely to have a greater influence, therefore there may be an even better case for openness (Birdsall & Wheeler present some evidence of this).

Wheeler & Martin (1992) show that in the pulp and paper industry, the more open the economy, the faster clean technology is adopted and diffused. They also show that a country's level of development has no independent effect on the adoption of clean technology. It may be that this is just a result for pulp and paper where the clean technology is also the cheapest, or that developing countries are not using cheaper more competitive pollution-intensive technology because the industry is led by industrialised countries who impose their clean technology on the developing country which result in cleaner technology than domestic preferences would imply.

Braga (1992) examines trade policy as a mechanism of resource management in the Indonesian and Brazilian forestry sectors, and argues that, contrary to environmentalists' beliefs, the use of export restrictions led to greater environmental degradation than a timber tax at the logging stage would have produced. The removal of tariff escalation practised by industrial countries is also argued as being more efficient and less environmentally degrading, in addition, proposed import embargoes on tropical hardwoods would also fail.

Overall, the link between trade, growth and environmental degradation is complex, it is positive for some forms of pollution but follows an inverted-U shape for others. Global market integration and outward-oriented policies promote the transfer of technology, specialisation and improved resource pricing. Such policies can lessen environmental degradation and accelerate the adoption of clean technology. Outward-oriented growth can also shorten the environmental transition period for developing economies by inducing larger income effects on the demand for environmental goods (Baldwin, 1993). Global integration of markets and international mobility of factors is also likely to promote a higher degree of co-ordination of domestic trade and environmental policies.

CGE analyses of the effects of trade liberalisation on environmental quality

Espinosa & Smith (1995) present a paper the purpose of which is to report the first generation of a composite non-market and CGE model for the EC, the United States, Japan and a single region for the rest of the world. The model incorporates morbidity and mortality effects of particulates, sulphur dioxides and nitrogen dioxides, and uses non-market valuation estimates with a specification for consumer preferences that allows changes in atmospheric emissions to diffuse in different amounts to each region, and have feedback effects on market demands. Since the ambient environment is treated as another mechanism (beyond markets) for interactions between economic agents, all policy interventions can, in principle, have market and non-market impacts on Hicksian welfare measures. The analysis presents both impacts by comparing the results of model specifications, with or without environmental feedback effects to evaluate trade liberalisation and environmental degradation scenarios.

The results indicate that the impact of environmental effects is minor when the policy scenario focuses on parameters linked to market transactions. When the mortality effects of pollution are included with those of morbidity, a more pronounced difference in the impact of removing trade barriers is seen. However, even without the mortality effects, the increased domestic production of durables induced by the substitution and income effects of reduced trade barriers, generates more pollution which in turn increases health costs and therefore the subsistence needs in the services sector. A reversal of the welfare effect was engineered by increasing the emission rate, this had a negative welfare effect even when excluding mortality effects. Overall, trade liberalisation is found to have a negative effect on the environment, but when accompanied by an environmental policy, it is found to be environmentally beneficial and welfare enhancing.

Beghin, Roland-Holst and van der Mensbrugghe (1995) analyse the environmental implications of growth and the opening up of trade in Mexico based on an empirical economy-wide model. In particular, they analyse how tradeoffs between growth and environmental objectives can be minimised by using targeted policies on pollution emissions in co-ordination with outward-oriented trade strategies. Pollution emissions in the model are linked by using polluting inputs rather than polluting outputs.

The results show economic integration will not exacerbate environmental degradation in Mexico and that the pollution elasticity with respect to growth is very stable in Mexico and not affected by trade. The new patterns of resource allocation, trade and production are found to be less pollution-intensive after trade liberalisation, however a strong scale effect dominates this and economic growth increases pollution in most sectors. It is concluded that environmental policy reforms that target the use of the polluting good are the best way to achieve pollution mitigation and that it would be appropriate to target a subset of sectors and pollutants, to lower administrative costs while achieving high abatement levels.

Perroni & Wigle (1994) present a general equilibrium model of the world economy with local and global environmental externalities, and use it to investigate the relationship between trade liberalisation and the environment. Their results show international trade has little effect on environmental quality and that the magnitude of the welfare effects of environmental policies is not significantly affected by changes in trade policy. They also find that size and distribution of the gains from trade liberalisation appear to be little affected by changes in environmental policies. It is argued that using trade policy for environmental objectives may be very costly as trade accounts for a small share of world production, a large share of trade is in environmentally clean goods, and pollution-intensive traded goods have abatement costs which are only a small percentage of total costs. Furthermore, even without environmental policy, trade liberalisation may promote a more efficient use of world resources.

Devarajan (1995) summarises that while there is theoretical backing for the proposition that pollution-intensive industries will migrate under free trade, the empirical evidence is somewhat mixed. Furthermore, the proposition is presented that even if dirty industries migrate, the solution to the problem is to improve pollution policies in the host country, not to prevent free trade.

— Chapter 3 —

Trade and Environment in New Zealand

Introduction

During the last few decades, widespread concern has developed at the national as well as the international level around issues related to environmental problems such as greenhouse gas emissions, ozone depletion, tropical deforestation, pollution of water resources and loss of biodiversity. These concerns regarding the quality of the environment have generated many questions regarding the interaction between trade and the environment. One such important question is the link between trade liberalisation and its effect on environmental quality.

New Zealand's situation with respect to this question is somewhat different and more complex than that for overseas situations. This is due to a combination of factors for which New Zealand is well-known.

- New Zealand's endowment of a clean, green natural environment contributes favourably to the development of agricultural, forestry and tourism industries. Furthermore these industries are of a high degree of importance to New Zealand (Hewison, 1995).
- The relatively high level of environmental awareness combined with the public's tradition of pride in the beauty of New Zealand, and commitment to protection of the environment (MfE, 1995).
- The international high profile as a small but independent nation that is prepared to stand strong on environmental issues such as drift-net

(purse-seine) fishing, whaling, ozone layer protection and nuclear energy (MfE, 1995).

- The withdrawal of subsidies for agriculture and liberalisation in other sectors since the mid-1980s, which has contributed to a range of economic and environmental benefits as well as the continued emphasis on further trade and investment liberalisation in the New Zealand government's economic strategy (Hewison, 1995).
- The introduction of innovative resource management policies, such as the Individual Transferable Quota system for sustainable fisheries, and the comprehensive and integrated Resource Management Act (RMA), the purpose of which is to promote sustainable management of natural and physical resources (MfE, 1995).
- The forestry, agricultural science, soil science, atmosphere and fisheries research institutes, which have a deserved reputation as international leaders (MfE, 1995).

Trade and environment issues have intensified in New Zealand in recent years. The article "New Zealand's Poisoned Paradise" which appeared in *New Scientist* in July 1993, although not entirely accurate, challenged New Zealand's reputation for environmental cleanliness, exposed the vulnerability of New Zealand's "clean, green" reputation, and heightened environmental concerns in New Zealand. The article expressed concern about the pollution created by waste timber treatment sites in a number of locations in New Zealand. Also in 1993, the Ministry for Agriculture and Fisheries published a report for the OECD on how New Zealand's environment benefited from trade liberalisation and the removal of agriculture subsidies.[1] This was a result of the fall in use of phosphate fertiliser, pesticides and less marginal land development following the removal of subsidies in 1986. These changes reduced off-farm contamination, especially of lakes and rivers, and restricted the degradation of newly developed land. The results suggest that by exposing agricultural production to market forces and international competition, better environmental outcomes can be obtained than with the use of subsidies and

[1]See Reynolds, R., Moore, W., Arthur-Worsop, M. and M. Storey (1993).

protectionism. Recently Fisher and Paykel (New Zealand whiteware producers) lobbied for an import ban on foreign fridges made using CFCs, since they produce CFC-free fridges that cost 6–10 per cent more. A ban was not imposed as it would have been inconsistent with GATT and would have offered little benefit in protecting the ozone layer, it may also have harmed future export opportunities. German recycling laws, standards for breakfast cereal additives, and indigenous people's intellectual property are further issues for New Zealand in the international trade and environment arena.

New Zealand has also been actively involved in environmental issues at the international level. New Zealand participated in international organisations such as GATT, OECD, UNCTAD, UNEP and Food and Agriculture Organisation of the United Nations (FAO), and treaties dealing with environmental concerns such as the Earth Summit organised by UNCED, the Montreal Protocol on Substances, the Framework Convention on Climate Change (FCCC) and the Convention on Biological Diversity (CBD) and has shown that it is a responsible member of the international community (Ratnayake, 1996).[2]

Geography of New Zealand

New Zealand is comprised of two large, and a number of smaller, islands located in the southwest Pacific Ocean between 33° and 55° south latitude. New Zealand is geographically isolated, relatively uncrowded and enjoys a unique endowment of natural resources such as water, coal and natural gas/petroleum. It has a combined land area of 270 500 km^2, is 1600 km long and spans 450 km at its widest point. At 11 500 km, it also has one of the longest, and in some places, most deeply indented coastlines in the world (MfE, 1994). The country sits astride the boundary of the Pacific and Indo-Australian tectonic plates and is known for its active volcanoes, geothermal areas and frequent earthquakes. This mountainous landscape and position on the Pacific "rim of fire" give New Zealand a wide diversity of natural

[2]See Williams (1995) for details on New Zealand's contribution to international environmental matters.

landscapes. Mountains are a significant part of the New Zealand landscape with more than three-quarters of the land area higher than 200 m above sea level. The temperate climate, which is a result of latitude and the proximity of the ocean, supports dense rainforest and lush grass. New Zealand's isolation as a remote island nation in the South Pacific protects it from the industrialised world's pollution. The relatively small local market (with a population of only 3.7 million people well-dispersed over the countries length) and few heavy industries, in a country similar in size to the United Kingdom or Japan, are the other main reasons for New Zealand's generally clear and unpolluted air. These factors, in conjunction with the beautiful scenery in areas such as Milford Sound, contribute to the "clean, green" international image (MfE, 1995).

Prior to human settlement, about 75 per cent of the country was covered by indigenous forest (MfE, 1994). Initially the Polynesian, and then the European, settlers each cleared about one-third of the original natural forest cover by burning and clearance for agriculture and it is now only 23 per cent covered (MfE, 1995). Forest clearance by Polynesians tended to be a slow process of fires and shifting agriculture, whereas clearance by European settlement from 1850 to about 1920 was much more rapid. Even though the pattern of land clearance was basically established by 1920, further (and sometimes controversial) clearance of natural forest continued until the mid-1980s, when the combined effects of conservation initiatives with the removal of land development subsidies mostly halted the activity. Nowadays about 80 per cent of natural forest resource is state-owned with the rest under private ownership (MfE, 1994). Virtually all state-owned natural forest is in national parks, forest parks and other reserves, with only around two per cent being managed for wood production (MfE, 1994). About 90 per cent of the private natural forests serve protective functions with the rest considered as commercially viable for sustainable wood production (MfE, 1994). Much of the country supports managed ecosystems, pasture, production forests and cropland. Farmland constitutes 66 per cent of the national land area and the 1.4 million hectares of sustainably managed planted forest provides almost 99 per cent of New Zealand's wood production, the predominant non-indigenous species being *Pinus radiata*

(MfE, 1994). Much of the vegetation and wildlife were unique, since the landmass drifted away from the ancient Gondwanaland around 100 million years ago. Flightless birds and other indigenous plants and animals were completely unprepared for the predators people brought with them. Since the advent of human settlement, half the endemic bird species have become extinct with over 400 species of indigenous birds, plants and animals listed as threatened. Furthermore, the quality of the native forest has been significantly damaged by introduced animals, particularly Australian possums and deer, and to a lesser extent goats and pigs.

New Zealand's economy

International trade has historically played an important role in New Zealand's economy. New Zealand was initially established as a colony to supply food and fibre to Britain and to serve as a market for British manufactured goods. To this day, New Zealand's economy remains heavily reliant on its natural resources. Although direct employment in primary industries is low (10.6 per cent) and falling, agriculture, fishing and forestry still provide the base for the manufacturing and processing industries. New Zealand's leading export sectors are predominantly agricultural and forestry products (see Figure 3.1). These make up almost 70 per cent of commodity export earnings, although exports from fishing, horticulture and manufacturing industries have also become significant. Livestock farming is integral to the New Zealand economy with about 70 million farm animals, mainly sheep and cattle. In 1993, meat exports were worth NZ$3.5 billion, dairy exports were NZ$3.3 billion, forest products were NZ$2.4 billion and wool exports exceeded NZ$1 billion as did fish exports. An important feature of these industries has been their management through "producer boards". In 1995, New Zealand's exports constituted 21 per cent of GDP and New Zealand held 0.3% of world trade. While this is not significant in overall world trade, in terms of world agricultural trade, New Zealand is considered an important player (MFAT, 1993). For example, New Zealand is far and away the largest sheepmeat exporter in the world, the second largest dairy exporter, and a significant exporter of beef. New Zealand also has a significant share

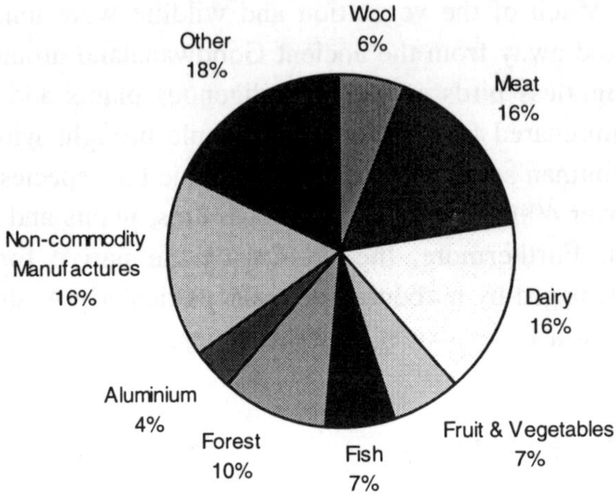

Figure 3.1 Major Exports as a Share of Total Exports (1992).
(*Source: MFAT, 1993*).

of the world market in horticulture, particularly in the export of kiwi fruit and apples. New Zealand's main export markets are Australia, the European Union, Japan, and the United States. Although typically seen as an agricultural nation, New Zealand does have some heavy industry, including a steel mill, an aluminium smelter, a synthetic petrol plant, cement works, and pulp and paper mills. Dairy factories and meat processing works are also spread throughout the country.

This century has been characterised by a period of pastoral domination of the economy followed by import-substitution, regulation and most recently deregulation of the economy (Hewison, 1995). During the 1960s and 1970s, New Zealand's economy was heavily protected, but during the last decade the New Zealand economy has undergone major restructuring designed to foster the development of an open, competitive and resilient economy (MfE, 1994). In 1984 following the election of the fourth Labour government, the country's internal conditions were not favourable. Poor growth, double-digit inflation, seven per cent fiscal and trade deficits, total external debt at 69 per cent of GDP, as well as a currency crisis all contributed to a rapid liberalisation in 1984. The basic policy was to deregulate entry and operating conditions, and to liberalise trade. A comprehensive agenda of both macro- and microeconomic reforms has resulted in the price system emerging as the dominant signal for agents' investment, production and consumption decisions. The major changes implemented include: removal of controls on prices, interest rates and wages; introducing a flexible exchange rate regime; giving the central bank (the Reserve Bank) independence to maintain price stability; achievement of fiscal surplus; extensive taxation reform aimed at reducing marginal rates and broadening the base; removal of agricultural subsidies and price supports; removal of quantitative import controls and ongoing tariff reductions; deregulation of oil, banking and transport markets; reform of labour market regulation; privatisation of State-Owned-Enterprises (SOEs); and wide-ranging public sector financial management reforms (MfE, 1994).

A number of these reforms have a limited, but not quantified, impact on carbon dioxide emissions. Examples include the removal of incentives and subsidies on the mining of coal and gas and the reform of the energy sector. In addition to these reforms, the New Zealand government has (since the early 1990s) also been actively pursuing a policy of sustainable agriculture, closely linked to the values of the RMA. The aim of this policy is to encourage and support farmers to move to more sustainable forms of agricultural production. In addition to focusing on agriculture, the New Zealand government has also been pursuing a policy of sustainable tourism. This long-term sustainability means serving anticipated visitor growth in a manner that meets the needs of present visitors, the needs of New Zealanders and protection of the natural resources and attractions upon which the industry is built (Hewison, 1995).

In terms of energy, New Zealand is self-sufficient in all but liquid fuels, importing around half its oil supplies. New Zealand's electricity generation is dominated by renewable energy sources, with hydroelectric power producing 70–75 per cent of annual needs, and geothermal another seven per cent (MfE, 1994).

The low density and dispersed nature of the New Zealand population has resulted in a significant dependence on private passenger vehicles as the dominant means of daily travel, as well as a low proportion of total commuters utilising public transport. Approximately 1.8 million passenger cars are registered to individuals in New Zealand. However, many fleet vehicles and some private vehicles operate on compressed natural gas (CNG) or liquid petroleum gas (LPG) which emit less carbon dioxide per kilometre travelled than petrol-fuelled vehicles.

Trade and Environment in New Zealand: Some Limited Evidence

The question of whether trade benefits or harms the environment is a demanding one for New Zealand, where government economic policy is based on a presumption that international trade will become more liberalised in the future. The New Zealand government's view is as follows:

> According to economic theory, the gains from trade are maximised when trade is not restricted. Global welfare will be improved by free trade between countries, allowing production to occur where the costs are lowest. This maximises the benefits that can be generated from a given set of resources. However, this requires that producers pay all costs, including environmental costs.[3]

Economic analysis of the relationship between trade and the environment in New Zealand is scarce.[4] One significant study of the impact of trade on the environment has been undertaken in New Zealand. The study was carried out by the Ministry of Agriculture and Fisheries (MAF) (1993) and examines the impact on the New Zealand environment of reduced agricultural subsidies in New Zealand for the period from 1975 to 1990.[5]

From 1975 to 1984, New Zealand maintained restrictive and managed economic policies as well as relatively high agricultural assistance levels,

---

[3]Hewison (1995), pp. 19–29.

[4]Because of the difficulty of obtaining environmental data, small open economies such as New Zealand have not been studied. However, a number of government agencies including Ministry of Foreign Affairs and Trade (MFAT), Ministry of Agriculture and Fisheries (MAF), and Ministry for the Environment (MfE), and researchers including Hewison (1995) have identified relevant issues for New Zealand.

[5]See Reynolds, R., Moore, W., Arthur-Worsop, M. and M. Storey (1993).

especially for pastoral farming, compared with other countries. In 1984, as part of the reforms to open the New Zealand economy, product price and farm input subsidies were removed. Most of the agricultural assistance that remained has since been dissociated from production and mostly consists of research, disaster relief and exit grants. The elimination of agricultural subsidies after 1984 had instantaneous effects on both farm inputs and outputs. In particular, the study notes that the use of phosphate fertiliser, pesticides and the rate of development of marginal lands (which was often indigenous forest) into pasture, declined substantially. The effects of these changes were to reduce the likelihood of off-site contamination, in particular water bodies and degradation of newly developed land. In addition, the environment benefited from a fall in sheep numbers and the diversification of pastoral farming away from sheep to deer, goats, horticulture and forestry, particularly from the reduced intensity of sheep grazing in certain hill country areas of New Zealand. The study found that agriculture liberalisation, in particular the removal of subsidies, resulted in some very positive environmental outcomes.

However, the study also noted that the legacy of poor land management practices in the past was still apparent. The study concluded that the liberalisation led to a cut in input use and stocking, but also meant farmers faced increasing income restraints. As a consequence, the farmlands vulnerability to the effects of droughts and storms has increased in certain areas. In many cases, farmers have lacked the income to adequately maintain land resources, invest in soil conservation, manage pests such as rabbits and possums, or convert marginal land into forestry. The vulnerability of certain farming areas to the effects of adverse climate conditions and degradation of land resources are problems that remain from the "development" (as opposed to "conservation")-oriented policies of the past.

A further important conclusion of the study is that the lessons learnt from the New Zealand experience also have international significance, especially since the agriculture sectors of most other OECD countries are much more heavily assisted and more intensive in their use of inputs than the New Zealand agriculture sector. It is suggested that non-production oriented assistance measures are likely to produce superior environmental outcomes than are production-oriented subsidies.

Another study by Ratnayake (1998) examines the relationship between environmental regulations and international competitiveness in New Zealand. Ratnayake considers the question of whether stringent environmental regulations lead to a loss of competitiveness in terms of declining exports and increasing imports in comparison to those from the nations with less stringent environmental regulations. The study is performed by undertaking an inter-industry analysis of New Zealand manufacturing industries. Ratnayake defines an international competitiveness measure and subsequently classifies industries as either environmentally sensitive or environmentally non-sensitive industries. Environmentally sensitive industries are defined as those that exhibit the highest pollution abatement costs as a percentage of output.

Overall, the revealed comparative advantage indices for New Zealand manufacturing exports indicate that the most competitive exports are in environmentally non-sensitive industries. Furthermore, by analysing the patterns of trade and revealed comparative advantage of New Zealand's trade with different country groups, Ratnayake shows that despite relatively high environmental standards, New Zealand's competitiveness in environmentally sensitive goods has not changed significantly over the years. Following the analysis of the patterns and determinants of comparative advantage of 109 industries over the last 13 years (1980 to 1993), no strong evidence is found to suggest that environmental standards have led to a loss of competitiveness in New Zealand manufacturing industries.[6]

Ratnayake (1999) is a collection of papers on some selected issues involved in the debate of trade and environment in the context of New Zealand. The first part of the book consists of some empirical studies which are inter-industry in nature. These studies attempt to test empirically various hypotheses on the linkages between trade and environment. The second

[6]An UNCTAD study calculated the degree of environmental stringency of a large number of countries and ranked countries on a scale of one (tolerant) to seven (strict) (Walter and Ugelow, 1979). The survey found the mean score for developed countries to be 6.1 while that of developing countries was 3.1. The environmental stringency index for New Zealand, Australia, Denmark, Germany and Netherlands was 5. The United States, United Kingdom and Sweden scored highest with a value of 7.

part is a collection of industry studies investigating the issues discussed in the first part at a sector or industry level. In one of these case studies, Sharp (1999) illustrates the linkages between property rights, trade and sustainable resource use. It has been shown that the management regime of regulated access coupled with subsidies contributed to serious depletion of high value fish stocks and minimal economic surplus in the fishing industry. Subsidies and non-transferable property rights had combined to produce unsustainable outcomes. However, an unprofitable fishing industry has been transformed to a dynamic profitable industry within the framework of rights-based fishing introduced since 1986. The study shows that in terms of biological sustainability and economic wealth in the fishery, the Quota Management System (QMS) easily out-performs regulated access.

Mikic (1999) explores the two-way relationship between agricultural trade and environment. Firstly, mechanisms and evidence for the impact of agricultural trade liberalisation on environmental quality are reviewed. Secondly, the impact of environmental policies on agricultural trade is examined. The paper provides a brief review on how the concerns on agriculture and environment have been handled in New Zealand, a leading country among the OECD members when it comes to elimination of assistance to agriculture. It has been concluded that in the case of agriculture, trade liberalisation in general results in improved economic efficiency and economic growth. On the other hand, it has been found that it is possible for environmental policies to weaken competitiveness and thus invoke renewed demand for protection.

Ratnayake (1999) examines some selected linkages of trade and environment in three environmentally sensitive manufacturing industries: plastics and synthetics, steel and paper. This investigation is based on a sample survey conducted in these three industries. According to the survey, the majority of firms are of the view that New Zealand's environmental regulatory system is very well-adapted or acceptable. It was also found that the RMA has little direct effect on output levels of companies participating in the survey. The cost of compliance in all industries was found to be insignificant in investment decisions of New Zealand. The majority of firms in the survey exported their goods to advanced developed countries where relatively high environmental standards are in place. The impact of environmental regulations on innovations was also examined. The question asked was how would firms respond to more stringent environmental regulations. Again the majority of firms stated that they would introduce new technologies to combat this constraint.

New Zealand's Trade and Environmental Policies

Since New Zealand has little overall influence in international trade and has a small domestic market of little significance to other countries, it has in recent years been a strong supporter of the multilateral trading system of the GATT where small countries like New Zealand can obtain the best outcomes. Because of this, the successful conclusion of the Uruguay Round and formation of the WTO should yield significant positive effects for New Zealand as a trading nation. New Zealand is committed to the overall direction of its economic and trade policy and as such it is unlikely to be altered.

A similar situation also exists with respect to the environment. Despite New Zealand being a small contributor to global environmental problems, it does however pride itself on being prominent in the international environmental arena, and furthermore, takes concern for the environment very seriously, particularly at the international level. In 1989 alone, New Zealand was represented by ministers at 14 major international meetings dealing with environmental issues (Hewison, 1995).

Up until the late 1980s, trade and environmental policies in New Zealand remained largely separate, with little attention paid to any interaction between the two. However, due to the international recognition of the need for reconciliation between these policies, the New Zealand government has begun a process of examining the interactions between both, in an effort to reach an equilibrium between the two. Despite New Zealand's size, multilateral negotiations offers many opportunities to play a significant role in international discussions on trade and the environment. However, because of New Zealand's limited resources it is necessary to carefully choose which of the many international meetings are the most important and the best ways to enhance its position (Hewison, 1995). The most obvious international forums are GATT, OECD, APEC and the International Standards Organisation (ISO), as well as UNCTAD and UNEP. Until recently, New Zealand's policy on trade and the environment was almost exclusively formulated by the MFAT, MAF and the Ministry of Commerce (MoC). Others such as the MfE, the Department of Conservation (DoC), and the Ministry of Forestry were involved only on the fringes. There has been little Cabinet consideration, but the government has now committed more resources to the issue. Hewison sees an immediate need for a more formal governmental inter-agency working group on trade and the environment. This could also be expanded at times into a larger structure — perhaps an informal council or conference — that includes representatives of public interest and industry Non-Governmental Organisations (NGOs). Formulation of an all-encompassing government policy will also require more extensive information sharing and reporting than is occurring at present.

Trade policy

The underlying objective of New Zealand's trade policy is to promote New Zealand's economic growth through trade and thus improve the living standards of New Zealanders on a sustainable basis (MFAT, 1993). New Zealand has adopted a four-track approach to trade policy (liberalisation): the unilateral track (domestic policy), the multilateral track (GATT), the regional track [APEC, Closer Economic Relations (CER)], and the bilateral track. The idea being not to rely solely on any one of the four. New Zealand recognises that the (theoretically) first-best option for New Zealand is complete multilateral free trade. Furthermore, by working within multilateral trade initiatives such as the GATT, the Cairns Group of Free Traders in Agriculture, and the OECD, New Zealand can help to develop an intellectual base for free trade, as well as trade and environment initiatives, and can, and have had, an influence on the design of international trade policy. However, New Zealand also recognises that regional trade initiatives (especially those incorporating open regionalism such as CER, APEC and PECC (Pacific Economic Cooperation Council) can be a step towards multilateral free trade. The policy of open regionalism has been adopted by the New Zealand government.

Trade liberalisation

Trade restrictions can be used to raise revenues for governments, to improve the balance of payments, and to protect domestic producers (Gale, 1990). In New Zealand, industry has historically been regulated and protected from international competition. The most common measures employed to achieve this protection have been tariffs, import licensing and export subsidies.[7] The combination of these various forms of protection led to very high levels of effective assistance up until the 1970s, approaching on average 70 per cent. Towards the end of the 1960s, the distortions caused by this protectionist system were causing greater concern than the revenue and protection afforded. However, it was not until 1979 that the process of reform was initiated. The reforms continued slowly until 1981 when pressure was exerted with respect to export subsidies via the GATT code on countervailing duties. Following the 1984 election of the fourth Labour government, a rapid programme of reform began. The Export Performance Tax Incentive (a tax credit of 14 per cent of value-added) was eliminated over three years and the Export Market Development Tax Incentive (a 150 per cent writeoff of development expenditure was phased out over six years. The most important export subsidy was the Supplmentary Minimum Price (SMP) guaranteed to farmers. This had become extremely expensive (exceeding NZ$400 million in 1983) and was finally abolished in 1984 and 1985 (Tyler & Lattimore, 1990). Import licensing, the primary instrument of protection in New Zealand until the 1980s was gradually removed and tariffs were subsequently reduced to 10–20 per cent by 1992. These changes resulted in the effective rate of assistance in manufacturing, for example, declining from 39 per cent in 1982 to 19 per cent in 1990 (Gale, 1990). Sectoral tariffs for 1990 can be seen in Table 3.1 below.

The trade agreement with Australia, CER, developed separately from the other reforms, with the emphasis on providing expanded markets for producers on both sides of the Tasman. The gains from the inter- and

[7]See Wooding, P. (1987).

Table 3.1 Tariffs by Sector (1990).

Sector	Tariff Rate % (*ad valorem*)	Sector	Tariff Rate % (*ad valorem*)
Dairy Farming	0.0	Non-Metallic	5.7
Sheep and Cattle	1.8	Basic Metals	3.8
Other Agriculture	0.6	Fabricated Metal	9.9
Fishing	0.0	Other Manufacturing	13.5
Forestry and Logging	0.0	Electricity etc.	0.0
Mining	0.0	Building	0.0
Dairy Processing	5.5	Trade, Restaurants and Hotels	0.0
Meat Processing	5.7	Transport	0.0
Other Food etc.	7.2	Communication	0.0
Textiles etc.	18.2	Finance etc.	0.0
Wood etc.	5.8	Dwellings etc.	0.0
Paper etc.	4.6	Private Services	0.0
Chemicals	6.9	Public Services	0.0

(*Source: Philpott and Nana, 1993*).

intra-industry trades are thought to exceed A$2 billion per year, or around 22 per cent of the value of the increased trade flows.[8]

Environmental policy

The *Environment 2010 Strategy*[9] states the vision for the New Zealand environment to 2010 as: "A clean, healthy and unique environment, sustaining nature and people's needs and aspirations", where the key conditions are, a competitive enterprise economy, effective laws and policies, information and social participation. The formation of environmental policy in New Zealand, as outlined in the *Environment 2010 Strategy*, follows eleven guiding principles including, principle 4 — the internalisation of external environmental costs, and principle 11 — protecting our international competitiveness.[10]

[8]Bureau of Industry Economics (1989).
[9]MfE (1995).
[10]See MfE (1995).

Principle 4 — the internalisation of external environmental costs, states: "Resource management should ensure that the unpriced environmental effects (or external costs) associated with the production, distribution and consumption of goods and services are "internalised", that is, they are assessed and constantly charged to users and consumers who benefit from them".

Principle 11, protecting our international competitiveness, states: "New Zealand will assist in protecting the international competitiveness of its businesses by improving its "clean, green" image, working with its trading partners to advance common interests, and playing a positive and active role internationally without getting out of step with other countries where this would significantly affect competitiveness". The goals and agenda for action refer to eleven priority issues for the New Zealand biophysical environment: managing land resources, managing water resources, maintaining clear, clean breathable air, protecting indigenous habitats and biological diversity, managing pests weeds and diseases, sustainable fisheries, managing the environmental impacts of energy services, managing the environmental effects of transport services, managing waste contaminated sites and hazardous substances, reducing the risk of climate change, and restoring the ozone layer (MfE, 1995).

New Zealand's carbon dioxide emissions policy

Climate change has, in recent years, emerged as an environmental issue that could have profound and lasting impacts on the planet. Addressing the issue of climate change is demanding, given our dependence on fossil fuels for economic activity and the need for governments to maintain and improve the quality of life for both present and future generations (MfE, 1994).

New Zealand's response to climate change was initiated in 1988 with the establishment of the New Zealand Climate Change Programme. This comprised of three working groups on climate change science, climate change impacts, and policy responses, and a fourth to ensure compliance with the Treaty of Waitangi.

In 1990, the Government established a target for reducing net emissions of carbon dioxide and began implementing initial policy measures. The target was to aim to reduce net carbon dioxide emissions to 20 per cent below their 1990 levels by the year 2000 conditional on the measures to achieve this objective being the most effective, providing the greatest range of benefits regardless of climate change, not reducing New Zealand's competitive advantage in international trade, and having a net benefit for New Zealand society (MfE, 1994). The initial policies adopted were limited to those that reduced carbon dioxide emissions or enhanced sinks while also being justified on grounds other than climate change (MfE, 1994).

New Zealand was an active participant in the negotiation of the FCCC. It was among the countries that signed the convention at the Earth Summit in June 1992. New Zealand ratified the FCCC on 18 September 1993, becoming the 34th Party to the Convention. New Zealand is committed to policy action as a signatory to the FCCC, the objective of which is to stabilise atmospheric concentrations of greenhouse gases at a level which avoids dangerous anthropogenic interference with the climate system (Working Group on CO_2 Policy, 1996). The FCCC also contains differentiated commitments for developed and developing countries, to reflect that developed countries have contributed most of the increase in levels of carbon dioxide in the atmosphere. New Zealand is one of the 36 Annex I Parties that have agreed to adopt national policies with the aim of returning anthropogenic emissions of greenhouse gases to 1990 levels. In 1995, the international community agreed current commitments were inadequate to achieve this objective, resulting in the Berlin Mandate which starts new negotiations for Annex I party commitments.

The government's policy responses have since been brought together under the Comprehensive Strategy on Climate Change, the purpose of which is to address sources and sinks of all greenhouse gases, and to help New Zealand adjust to the impacts of climate change.[11]

Upon the formation of the Comprehensive Strategy on Climate Change, New Zealand also established a domestic carbon dioxide target consistent with the FCCC. New Zealand's primary carbon dioxide objective is to take precautionary actions to help stabilise atmospheric concentrations of carbon

---

[11]This does not include those covered by the Montreal Protocol.

dioxide, in order to reduce risk from global climate change and to meet New Zealand's commitments under the FCCC. Specifically, to return net emissions of carbon dioxide to no more than their 1990 levels by the year 2000 (but to aim for reduction in net carbon dioxide emissions to 20 per cent below their 1990 levels by the year 2000 if this is cost-effective, will not harm our international trade, and has a net benefit to New Zealand society) and to maintain them at this level thereafter (MfE, 1995). The net target derives from offsetting carbon absorption by planted forests against gross carbon dioxide emissions.

Policies and measures to limit emissions and enhance sinks

The government has implemented a range of policy measures to reduce carbon dioxide emissions in 2000, these are complemented by the significant increase in carbon absorption sinks that will result in New Zealand's net emissions falling below their 1990 level by 2000.[12] The policy package consisted of three main components:

(1) Emissions reduction: 20 per cent of the reductions required to meet the target were to be met through various measures described below, including voluntary actions, the RMA and deregulation of the energy sector.

(2) Additional carbon absorption: 80 per cent of the reductions required to meet the target were forecast to be met through increases in planted forestry.

(3) A low-level carbon charge was to be introduced in December 1997 if, on analysis, the two previous measures do not seem likely to result in the target being met.

In an attempt to reduce gross carbon dioxide emissions, a number of policy measures have been introduced by the New Zealand government:

[12]See MfE (1994) for a more detailed explanation of the policies adopted by the New Zealand government to reduce net carbon dioxide emissions.

- Use of the RMA (1991) as a regional tool to consider carbon dioxide emissions in plans, policy statements and resource use consents, in particular by requiring resource consents for large stationary emitters.
- Energy sector regulatory reforms (deregulation) to establish a more competitive wholesale electricity market.
- The Energy Efficiency Strategy pursuing a ten-point strategy through the Energy Efficiency and Conservation Authority (EECA), to facilitate the uptake of cost-effective energy-efficient practices and technologies, and overcome barriers to renewable energy resources.
- Co-operative energy efficiency programmes between the EECA and industrial and commercial firms, and public sector organisations such as schools and hospitals etc.
- Removal of barriers to encourage greater uptake of renewable sources of energy, particularly wind and biomass.
- Voluntary agreements with industry to promote increased energy efficiency and conservation, and greater use of renewable energy in order to reduce carbon dioxide emissions.
- Specific transport measures including taking carbon dioxide into account in regional transport strategies and road funding. As well as the Land Transport Pricing Study which has the potential to result in improved efficiency of the land transport sector, especially through pricing and by altering demand or patterns of use of different modes of transport.

In addition to these measures in the year 2000, New Zealand's planted forests are projected to remove 25 519 gigagrams (Gg) of carbon dioxide from the atmosphere (MfE, 1994). Carbon stored in natural and planted forests in New Zealand is at least 100 times greater than the net annual carbon absorption level. The forests are therefore a substantial carbon reservoir as well as a significant carbon sink (MfE, 1994). In 1994, the new forest planting could reach 135 000 hectares. An average of 100 000 hectares of new forest is expected to be planted each year at least until 2005 (MfE, 1994).

The New Zealand government has also introduced a number of policy measures that are expected to reduce net carbon dioxide emissions by increasing carbon sinks.

- The adoption of a number of policies to promote the expansion of commercially planted forests.
- The East Coast forestry project, which aims to plant 200 000 hectares of commercially productive forest over the next 28 years.
- The introduction of a number of measures to protect indigenous forests and to eliminate unsustainable forestry management practices.
- The adoption of a "risk averse" approach to management of the national forest estate.

Working group on CO_2 policy

In 1996, the Working Group on CO_2 Policy published a discussion document entitled "Climate Change and CO_2 Policy: A Durable Response". The Working Group was established in August 1995 to examine how New Zealand can best meet the twin objectives of stabilising net carbon dioxide emissions at 1990 levels by the year 2000, and at the same time, minimising the impacts and risks to economic output and growth (Working Group on CO_2 Policy, 1996). It analyses several alternative approaches to achieving these objectives, including the use of economic instruments. The Working Group was specifically required to assess: the appropriateness of the processes of the RMA for addressing the global phenomena of climate change, and for determining New Zealand's compliance with its international commitments to stabilise carbon dioxide emissions; the appropriateness of New Zealand pursuing an emissions reduction target in net terms, and whether a carbon charge is the most efficient economic instrument for achieving the government's carbon dioxide objectives (Working Group on CO_2 Policy, 1996).

The Working Group provides the following conclusions with respect to the development of carbon dioxide emissions policy in New Zealand:

- Approaches to reducing carbon dioxide emissions should be least cost, preserve maximum flexibility in terms of responses, be part of a global response, and be durable both domestically and internationally.

- Policies must promote the widest range of options for reducing emissions, so least-cost actions would be apparent and implemented first, and thus allowing government and emitters the most flexibility in managing uncertainties.
- Should the government wish to move further towards its policy target, or move beyond it in the future, then an economic instrument [in the form of charges or tradable carbon certificates (TCCs)] provides the least-cost means of reducing emissions. Including both emissions and absorption (i.e. a net carbon dioxide emissions target) would maximise the opportunities for least-cost abatement responses.
- Specific subsidies or regulatory interventions will not, in general, provide a least-cost or durable response to reducing carbon dioxide emissions.
- New Zealand should advocate the introduction of economic instruments internationally so that the price of carbon is increased on a comparable basis across all Annex I countries. This would encourage the widest range of technological and other responses, lower the total costs of global abatement, and facilitate the progressive inclusion of non-Annex I countries.
- Achieving the stabilisation target or any substantial reduction in emissions will be costly for all Annex I countries including New Zealand. To minimise trade and investment distortions in achieving the desired environmental outcome, all Annex I countries, including New Zealand, should move broadly in line with each other.
- To provide a long-term, durable, least-cost response, and to support New Zealand's advocacy of such an approach internationally, the government should endorse as its intended instrument, a TCC scheme (including both emissions and absorption of carbon dioxide capped with an optional carbon charge to manage volatility and overall cost and progress work on design and implementation details to confirm its feasibility.
- The government should improve the measure of carbon storage, particularly in indigenous forests.
- A decision should be made by 2000 on settings and timing of implementation of the TCC scheme, based on Annex I countries

moving to the introduction of measures of comparable marginal cost. This would not be before the conclusion of the Berlin Mandate negotiations.

- New Zealand should continue with the current policy, in the interim, but any carbon charge should not be increased beyond a low level prior to the introduction of the TCC scheme.
- A nationally legislated economic instrument, operated at a level sufficient to meet New Zealand's FCCC commitments, would remove the rationale for declining or attaching conditions to a consent in respect of carbon dioxide, or any rationale for a National Policy Statement under the RMA.[13]

Carbon dioxide emissions in New Zealand

Gross carbon dioxide emissions

In 1990, New Zealand emitted 25 530 Gg of carbon dioxide (Chivers, 1995).[14] Emissions of carbon dioxide from the combustion of fossil fuels made up approximately 90 per cent of New Zealand's emissions, with the remainder attributable to industrial processes. The transport sector is the largest source of carbon dioxide emissions in New Zealand accounting for 34 per cent of total carbon dioxide emissions in 1990 (MfE, 1994).

[13] Working Group on CO_2 Policy (1996), p. 9.

[14] The FCCC requires parties to provide inventories of their anthropogenic greenhouse gas emissions by source and removals by sinks. The agreed base year for the inventories is 1990. Estimates are made in accordance with Intergovernmental Panel on Climate Change (IPCC) draft guidelines. The estimates of carbon dioxide emissions from energy use have a degree of uncertainty ± 5 per cent, but do not include those from industrial processes for iron, steel, aluminium, cement and lime production, or those from natural sources. The IPCC defines energy emissions as "total emissions of greenhouse gases from energy activities (this includes fuel combustion as well as fuel production, transport, storage and distribution but not emissions from the combustion of wood and related products)". It is assumed in any case, that for New Zealand, wood used for energy is sourced from planted forests that are continually replanted and that in the long run produce no net emissions (Chivers, 1995). In New Zealand, planted forests are actually a sink, i.e. more carbon is absorbed by forests than is released by them.

A strong correlation between growth in energy consumption, and hence carbon dioxide emissions, and the rate of economic growth exists. For every ten per cent increase in GDP, there was a six per cent increase in gross emissions (Working Group on CO_2 Policy, 1996). Since 1990, there has been a significant increase in gross emissions from energy sources and industrial processes and, in the absence of any further policy measures, current projections are for gross emissions to increase 22–25 per cent between 1990 and the year 2000 (see Table 3.3 and Figure 3.4) (Working Group on CO_2 Policy, 1996). However, it is projected that the share of emissions among sectors would remain fairly constant (Figure 3.2) (MfE, 1994). Although New Zealand's gross carbon dioxide emissions are projected to increase, the current emissions profile is relatively low due to the substantial contribution of renewables in the production of energy (75 per cent of electricity needs). While there is scope to develop further renewable energy capacity,

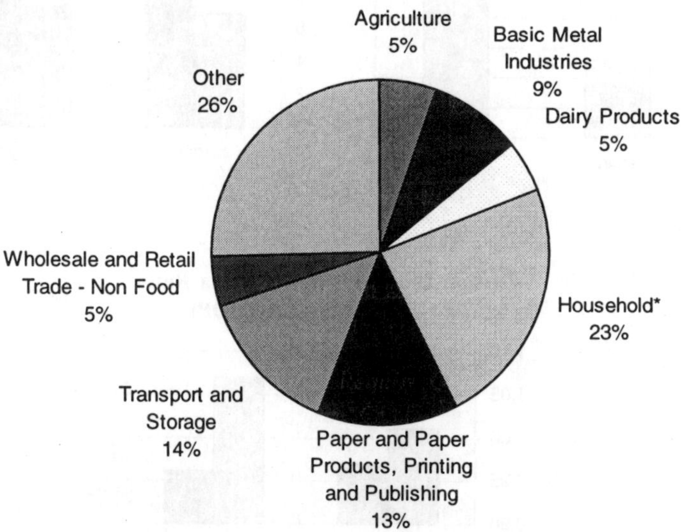

Figure 3.2 Carbon Dioxide Emissions by Sector (1991/1992).
NB: Household* includes domestic transport, of which carbon dioxide emissions from petrol consumption amount to ten per cent of all emissions.
(*Source: Ministry of Commerce*).

Table 3.2 Comparison of Carbon Dioxide Emissions from Energy Statistics 1990–1992.

	CO_2 Emissions Growth	Per Capita Emissions		Emissions-GDP Ratio	
	1990–1992	1990	1992	1990	1992
New Zealand	+8.3%	6.9	7.4	1.01	1.07
OECD Average	+0.7%	11.8	11.7	0.97	0.96
Rank	23	7	10	7	12

(*Source: Chivers, 1995*).

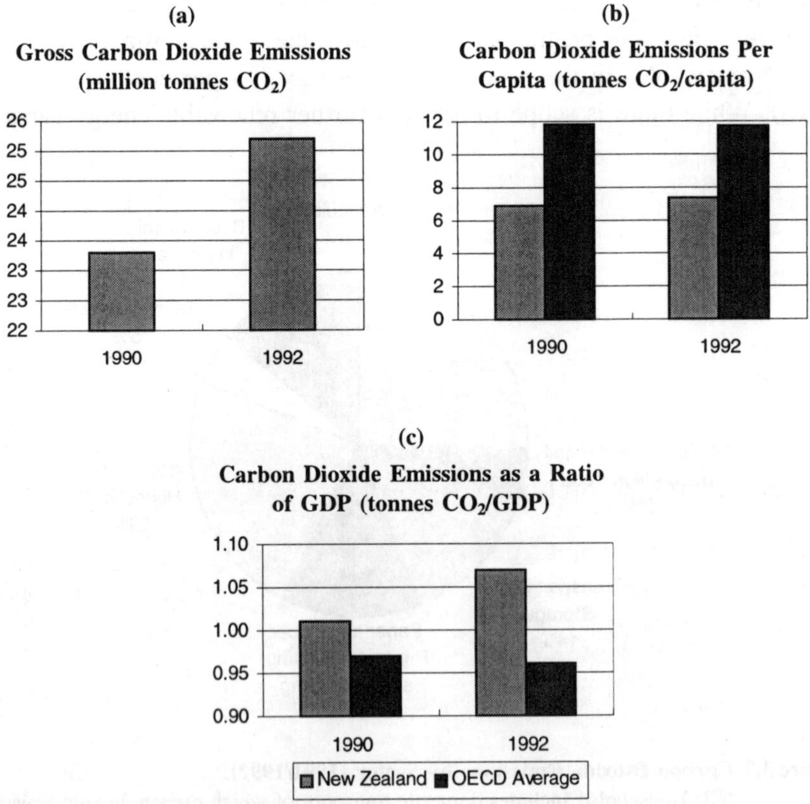

Figure 3.3 New Zealand-OECD Comparison of Carbon Dioxide Emissions 1990/1992. (*Source: Chivers, 1995*).

particularly wind power, predicted future energy requirements mean some increase in power generation from fossil fuels is necessary (MfE, 1994).

New Zealand's carbon dioxide emissions growth, per capita emissions and emissions-GDP ratio can be compared with the average for OECD countries.[15]

New Zealand had the second largest rate of growth in carbon dioxide emissions from energy in the OECD from 1990 to 1992 (Chivers, 1995). Table 3.2 shows New Zealand's growth rate is much higher than the OECD's average of 0.7 per cent.[16] Gross carbon dioxide emissions levels can be seen in Figure 3.3(a).

In 1990, New Zealand ranked seventh out of the 24 OECD countries by carbon dioxide emissions per capita. By 1992, New Zealand's ranking had fallen to tenth as emissions per capita were seven per cent higher than in 1990 (Chivers, 1995). Nevertheless, New Zealand remained well below the OECD average, see Table 3.2 and Figure 3.3(b).

New Zealand ranked seventh out of the OECD countries in 1990 in terms of carbon dioxide emissions as a ratio of GDP (in 1985 US$), at four per cent above the OECD average. New Zealand fell to twelfth place in 1992, as emissions as a ratio of GDP grew to 11 percent above the OECD average, which had dropped slightly over the period (Chivers, 1995), see Table 3.2 and Figure 3.3(c).

Carbon dioxide absorption

Forestry absorption of carbon dioxide was estimated at 16 716 Gg in 1990 (MfE, 1994).[17] This figure takes into account an estimated 1255 Gg

[15]Data for other OECD countries are taken from Tables 5 and 6 of *Climate Change Update 1994*, published by the International Energy Agency (IEA).

[16]It should be noted that there was a large increase in emissions in 1992 due to a hydroelectricity shortage, which meant fossil fuels were used to a greater degree in the production of energy. If this comparison is repeated for 1993, New Zealand improves a few places but is still well above the OECD average.

[17]See MfE (1994) for details on how this sink figure is arrived at.

of carbon dioxide that was emitted through forest clearing and fires. Current absorption estimates focus mainly on changes in planted forests, although emissions from indigenous forest harvesting, fires and scrub clearance for forestry are included. The results of a survey of new planting intentions are for approximately 70 000 hectares per annum to the year 2000 and 55 000 hectares per annum to 2010 of projected plantings (Working Group on CO_2 Policy, 1996). The combined effects of the reduction in expected new planting rates and refinements to the emissions projection model mean that, based on current policy, New Zealand cannot presently expect carbon absorption by planted forests to do much more than maintain the level of 1990 absorption by the year 2000 (Working Group on CO_2 Policy, 1996). However, it must be noted that considerable uncertainty to this work remains, and that the coverage of current absorption data is not complete.

Net carbon dioxide emissions

Net emissions are calculated as gross emissions less any net absorption by forest sinks. Current projections indicate that, in the absence of any further policy measures, New Zealand will not stabilise net emissions at 1990 levels by the year 2000, see Table 3.3 and Figure 3.4 (Working Group on CO_2 Policy, 1996). Net emissions are projected to increase by 61 per cent (from 7.7 million tonnes in 1990 to 12.5 million tonnes in 2000), although the absence of data on forest reversion on marginal land, changes in the indigenous forests, and soil carbon introduces considerable uncertainty (Working Group on CO_2 Policy, 1996). This projection differs to that made by MfE (1994) and is mainly because of higher projected GDP growth rates, causing increased emissions growth, and significantly lower levels of new planting this decade than anticipated, which reduces absorption in the future.[18]

[18]Note that these projections are very sensitive to the estimates of projected GDP growth rates and new planting estimates.

Table 3.3 Net Carbon Dioxide Emissions: Estimates 1990–1994 and Projections to 2010.

	1990	1991	1992	1993	1994	2000	2005	2010
Gross Emissions	25.5	26.0	27.9	27.3	27.4	31.1	33.6	36.3
Absorption	−17.7	−15.8	−15.1	−14.8	−13.8	−18.6	−23.5	−25.1
Net Emissions	7.8	10.1	12.9	12.5	13.7	12.5	10.1	11.2
Change in Net Emissions (relative to 1990)		+31%	+65%	+60%	+76%	+61%	+30%	+44%

Note: Carbon dioxide absorption is by international convention, presented as negative since it represents a removal of carbon dioxide from the atmosphere. Figures are in millions of tonnes of carbon dioxide and are actual emissions for 1990–1994 and projections for 2000–2010.
(*Source: Working Group on CO_2 Policy, 1996*).

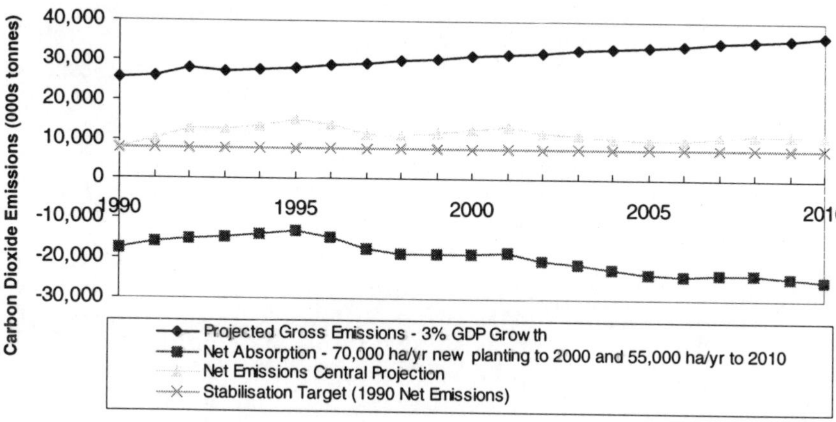

Note: Net absorption and hence net emissions, does not include any allow ance for forest reversion, natural forest degradation, non-forestry land clearance or changes in soil carbon.

Figure 3.4 Projected Carbon Dioxide Emissions: Sources and Sinks.
(*Source: Working Group on CO_2 Policy, 1996*).

Summary

The recent intensification of interest in environmental matters in New Zealand has, in combination with New Zealand's reliance on environmental quality to maintain it's international "clean, green" image, raised the profile of the trade and environment debate in New Zealand. The article in *New*

Scientist and the OECD's call for co-ordinated trade and environment policies has further augmented the emphasis on trade and environment issues in New Zealand. These issues are particularly relevant for New Zealand due to the heavy dependence on international trade, and the progressive removal of trade-related protectionist measures. New Zealand has recently introduced innovative environmental policies which promote sustainability. Furthermore, New Zealand is expected to implement a carbon tax in order to ensure it meets its carbon dioxide emissions reduction commitments under the FCCC. These factors, in conjunction with the present lack of trade- and environment-related studies on New Zealand, mean that an investigation of the likely effects of trade liberalisation on welfare and carbon dioxide emissions both in the absence, and presence, of a carbon tax is particularly pertinent.

— Chapter 4 —

A Trade and Environment Focused Multisectoral CGE Model

Introduction

The majority of the literature on trade and the environment is theoretical in nature with most analyses agreeing that trade policies are a poor substitute for domestic environmental policies and that trade liberalisation and environmental protection can be treated as separate objectives.[1] However there has been very little attention paid to the empirical or computable quantification of these results.[2]

This study is an attempt to assess the magnitude of the effects of trade liberalisation on welfare and emissions levels, and the degree to which these effects are influenced by environmental policy. This study will concentrate on these effects within the New Zealand economy, however the results obtained will be widely applicable to other small open market-based economies. The results of this study will assist in providing a prescription for New Zealand's trade and environmental policies and should help to fill some of the empirical vacuum in this field. It is expected based on theoretical analyses, that the results will show trade liberalisation to be welfare-enhancing, and for it to have a minimal impact on environmental quality in the presence of environmental policies which internalise environmental externalities.

[1]See for example Bhagwati (1981).

[2]For a survey of empirical studies, see Dean (1992) and Beghin, Roland-Holst & van der Mensbrugghe (1994). CGE studies have been undertaken by Perroni and Wiggle (1994), Smith & Espinosa (1994, 1995) and Beghin, Roland-Holst & van der Mensbrugghe (1995).

Because the questions raised in this study have economy-wide implications, this study assesses the consequences of trade and environmental policies using a computable general equilibrium (CGE) model for the New Zealand economy incorporating a trade and environment focus.

The advantage of CGE models over other empirical models is that they can capture the numerous complex relationships between variables in the model economy, many of which may not be apparent or expected before the analysis. The usefulness of a general equilibrium approach can be seen in the analysis of second-best situations. One recent example of this concerns the argument for trade restrictions as opposed to environmental policy as a means of protecting the environment.[3] This question is easily examined in a general equilibrium context and the results of the two policies not only on the environment, but also on the rest of the economy, can be compared. Furthermore, only a general equilibrium evaluation of these policies can assess the impacts of their respective effects on welfare.[4]

This chapter presents the multisectoral general equilibrium trade and environment model developed for the analysis in this study. The model is relatively simple and closely follows neoclassical theory, however inter-industry linkages, sectoral protection, and sectoral emissions are explicitly modelled. The model that will be employed is in part based on the work of Jaime de Melo & David Tarr (1992), who have developed a CGE model for the United States economy to analyse the effects of trade liberalisation under various scenarios. By using a similar type of model but specifically including the environment (in the form of emissions), it will be possible to achieve a detailed and precise analysis of trade liberalisation's environmental effects in New Zealand, and whether it remains a welfare-enhancing policy change. This analysis is performed both with and without an emissions tax to evaluate trade liberalisation and environmental degradation scenarios.[5]

---

[3]This may occur because some countries may not be able to implement an environmental policy effectively due to political or enforcement problems.

[4]See Borges (1986) for a summary of the advantages and disadvantages of CGE models.

[5]The emissions tax is levied against carbon dioxide emissions and is essentially the same as the carbon tax to be implemented in New Zealand in the near future. Here the terms emissions tax and carbon tax will be used interchangeably.

Two policy scenarios will be examined by this study:

(1) The effects of trade liberalisation will be examined in the absence of a carbon tax.
(2) The effects of trade liberalisation will be examined in the presence of a carbon tax.

The Model

Overview of the model

The model introduced here is a simple neoclassical model for a small open economy, focusing on international trade and the environment. The model is designed to analyse the long-run effects of trade liberalisation on welfare and the level of carbon dioxide emissions both within and without the presence of an emissions tax. Since the focus is on the effects of trade and environmental policies, and not on policy issues related to investment decisions, unnecessary complication is avoided by not modelling the investment decision. Similarly, the consumption decisions of the government are not modelled. Thus all final domestic demand for the output of a sector is treated as private consumption demand. Total domestic demand for the output of a sector is the sum of domestic intermediate demand plus domestic consumption demand. It is also assumed that all consumers have identical preferences so that their behaviour is modelled by a "representative" consumer. The government collects tariffs and environmental taxes, where the government's budget surplus is distributed to the consumer as a lump sum payment.[6] The single representative consumer purchases domestic and foreign goods and maximises utility, given income and prices. The consumer's income is determined endogenously. At any set of prices, consumer expenditures on commodities equals consumer money income inclusive of transfers. The latter property means that the model satisfies

[6]Since both tariffs and environmental taxes cannot be negative then the government budget cannot be in deficit. It is therefore assumed the following inequality holds throughout, $G \geq 0$.

Walras' law. Since demand functions have homogeneity of degree zero, then only relative prices are of significance for domestic agents.

The exchange rate is flexible and is assumed to adjust to maintain the current account position, expressed in foreign units, which remains unchanged as a result of policy simulation. Thus any exogenously given current account deficit that exists in the year for which the model is benchmarked will continue to prevail after the policy simulation. This treatment of the current account guarantees that there will be no permanent capital transfers taken from, or given to, the rest of the world in the policy simulations. This assumption makes welfare analysis of changes in policy more meaningful and transparent.

The model is general equilibrium in the sense characterised by Arrow & Debreu (1954). Producers maximise profits subject to constant returns to scale technology. Given technology, and output and input prices, the representative firm in each industry purchases primary factors and domestic and foreign intermediate inputs so as to minimise the costs of producing a level of output. The production technology for value-added factors is described by a neoclassical production function that allows smooth substitution between inputs. The degree of substitution is governed by the elasticities of substitution specified. The most important question in this context relates to the degree of substitutability one believes ought to be specified. For most purposes in economy-wide modelling, it can be reasonably argued that the use of constant elasticity of substitution (CES) production functions with realistic substitution elasticities will capture most of the interactions one wants to analyse.

Intermediates from different sectors, as well as emissions, enter production with a fixed coefficient (Leontief) technology. Existing CGE models have often retained the assumption of fixed coefficients for intermediate technology.[7] This choice of functional forms has the practical advantage of reducing considerably the number of parameters necessary for implementing the model. In terms of neoclassical production functions, this specification

---

[7]In virtually all applications an inter-industry table is used, and intermediates from different sectors usually enter with a fixed coefficient (Leontief) technology (De Melo & Tarr, 1992).

of production technology seems cumbersome. Mathematically, a generalised or multilevel CES function would have been more consistent. There is however, an advantage to this fixed coefficient (Leontief) specification. Specifying more elaborate production functions leads to a proliferation of parameters that must be estimated. Parameter estimation has always been a difficult problem in economy-wide planning models, and it is necessary to consider the tradeoffs between adequate econometric estimation and adequate structural specification (Dervis, de Melo & Robinson, 1982). However, these modelling assumptions, while defensible, are not harmless, the result being a reduced scope for substitution possibilities. Given the necessity of aggregating sectors in any applied economy-wide model into a relatively small number, it should be made quite clear that the production functions are only very approximate representations of actual technical production processes. Despite this, they remain an extremely flexible and convenient tool, and their sensible use at the sectoral level is unlikely to significantly distort the representation of the underlying technology.

In the light of other similar studies, the particular specifications used in this study seem to be empirically reasonable for the level of aggregation and the types of issues being examined. It is reasonable to assume that the amount of capital in each sector is fixed at the beginning of the period being modelled, but since we are interested in finding an equilibrium configuration for some future year without actually modelling the path to it, then it is sensible to allow the model to determine sectoral capital stocks endogenously. The specification of the production set of the economy is incomplete without factor availability restraints, here we assume capital and labour stocks are fixed. Each sector of the economy is treated as made up of many similar firms maximising profits and bidding for the scarce factors. We assume producers maximise profits and that demanders minimise the cost of purchasing a given quantity of composite good. These assumptions lead to the composite good price equations and the ratio equations, and are effectively dual unit cost functions.[8] Because agents are profit maximisers

[8]De Melo & Tarr (1992).

or cost minimisers, the functions describing the model are homogeneous of degree zero in prices.

A general equilibrium results when all industries are in equilibrium, all product and factor markets clear, and the current account expressed in foreign units equals its initial value. Given the properties described above, a general equilibrium is known to exist, and since preferences are reduced to a representative consumer, the resulting equilibrium is unique.[9] The model is required to replicate an historic dataset, in this case 1990, as an initial equilibrium. Determining the parameter values that (together with the observed data set) lead to this initial equilibrium of the model is known as benchmarking, or calibrating, the model. This process is described in detail in Appendix A. Once the model is calibrated, the exogenous policy variables can then be manipulated to simulate trade liberalisation and environmental policy, with the resulting new equilibrium showing the effects of these policy changes in the economy.

Finally, it should be emphasised that an applied CGE model cannot be seen as a short-run projection model and is not intended for that purpose. It is better suited to explain medium to long-run trends and structural responses to changes in policy. This is not to say the CGE model should not produce good predictive performance. In fact, they should be able to predict, conditional upon policy variables, trends in sectoral structure, inter-sectoral terms of trade, and trade performance, and do so more consistently than linear models or more informal methods.

Aggregation

For analysing the effects of trade liberalisation and carbon dioxide emissions, the economy is aggregated into five sectors: agriculture and food, textiles apparel and leather, chemicals, manufactures and services. This aggregation was chosen because it enables the isolation of separate industries in the model which are of significance in terms of trade restrictions and emissions levels. Furthermore, accurate data is readily available for these

[9]See Arrow & Hahn (1971).

industry classifications. Since both the average level of protection and the dispersion of protection across sectors contribute to the cost of protection, in principle it is always preferable to disaggregate further.[10] However, disaggregation is difficult in an economy-wide context, as it is often difficult to obtain reliable elasticity estimates. For assessing the costs of protection in the textiles and apparel and manufacturing sectors, and emissions in the agriculture, manufacturing and chemical sectors, this aggregation is adequate as these sectors remain explicitly treated, isolated sectors of the economy.[11]

Substitution elasticity specification

The functional forms used in the model are summarised in Figures 4.1(a) and (b). Starting with foreign trade, we treat the products produced by New Zealand and the rest of the world as differentiated, where the functional forms for import demand are CES, as explained below.

Production substitution possibilities utilise two-level nesting. At the first level is a Leontief input-output production function, where firms use a composite of primary factors of production, emissions and *n* composite intermediate inputs, one from each sector. At the second level each of the composite functions is defined. The primary factor of production is a composite of two primary factors, capital and labour, which substitute smoothly for each other through CES value-added functions. The parameters of the CES vary across sectors. Each sector uses intermediate inputs, where these inputs come from both domestic and foreign sources. Intermediate inputs from a given sector are sourced from domestic and foreign intermediate inputs. These intermediate goods enter production with fixed coefficients (Leontief technology). Emissions also enter into each sector's production in the form of a non-traded intermediate input.

---

[10]It is well-known that the costs of protection are a function not only of average tariff levels but also of their dispersion, see Johnson (1960).

[11]The costs of protection as well as emissions are assessed for all sectors, however these industries exhibit the highest levels of protection and emissions respectively.

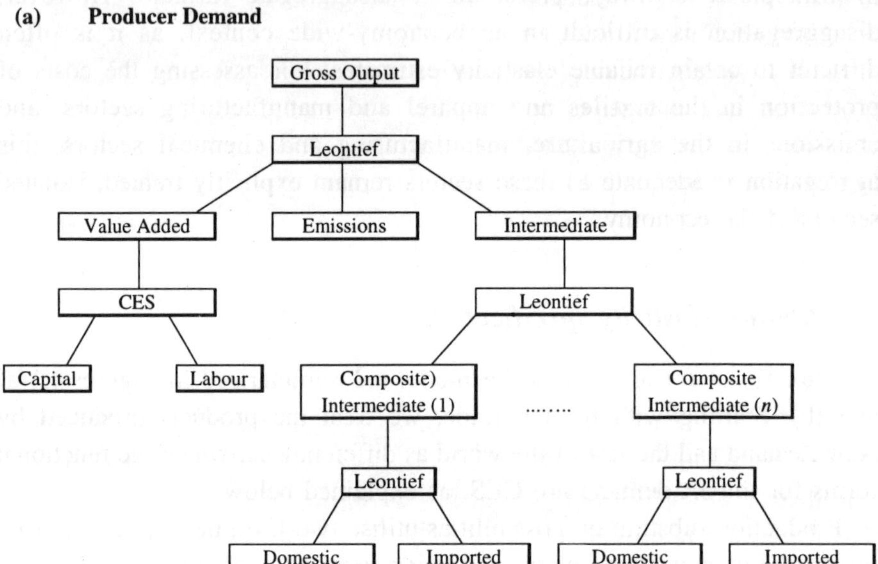

Figure 4.1 Demand Structure and Elasticity Specification.

For consumption demand, a Stone-Geary linear expenditure system (LES) allows for cross price effects in demand. Substitution possibilities between domestic and foreign produced goods of the same category are represented by nested CES functions.

A final issue is whether New Zealand would face fixed terms of trade for the trade policy changes to be modelled. This study's view is that in most cases the small country assumption for New Zealand in world markets is a good first order approximation. However it is also assumed that New Zealand would face a non-infinite foreign elasticity of demand for its agricultural exports.[12]

Modelling international trade

The treatment of imports

Most recent multisectoral CGE models assume national product differentiation, that is, products from different regions or nations are not identical.[13] Under constant returns to scale technology and perfect competition, these models rely on the assumption that domestically and foreign produced goods are imperfect substitutes, in order to overcome the "specialisation" problem.[14] The assumption of imperfect substitution is required because sectoral aggregation in the presence of only a few primary factors of production would lead to extreme specialisation if domestically and foreign produced goods were perfect substitutes.

When a country's share in the world market is very small, and when users do not differentiate products by country or region of origin, a country is like a small firm in a competitive market, it is a price taker and cannot

[12]Though New Zealand is not significant in overall world trade, the country is considered an important player in terms of world agricultural trade (MFAT, 1993). For example, New Zealand is far and away the largest sheep meat exporter in the world, the second largest dairy exporter and a significant exporter of beef and horticulture (particularly kiwi fruit and apples).

[13]De Melo & Tarr (1992).

[14]The specialisation problem arises because CGE models with a foreign trade focus are usually designed to estimate the welfare cost of trade distortions, which requires a reasonable degree of sectoral disaggregation in order to capture the costs of dispersion in protection across sectors.

affect the terms at which it trades. The small country assumption is very hard to reconcile with observed facts, and the assumption of perfect substitutability in use between foreign and domestic goods rules out the possibility of two way trade ignoring transport and storage costs.[15] Furthermore, perfect substitutability implies that the "law of one price" will hold, where the world price determines the domestic price.[16] This problem increases with the level of aggregation in the model, and most applied models require a fair degree of aggregation. In models focusing on trade policy and its effects, the perfect substitutability assumption greatly exaggerates the influence of trade policy on the domestic price system and economic structure. For example in the textiles sector, perfect substitutability implies there will either be imports or exports but never both, and that changes in world prices are fully translated into domestic prices. Thus in a country where textile imports are mainly cotton and domestic production is mainly synthetics, the small country assumption implies that a 50 per cent increase in the import price of cotton will lead to a 50 per cent increase in the domestic price of synthetics. Disaggregation is the best way around this problem, but it is not empirically possible to implement an economy-wide general equilibrium model distinguishing a couple of hundred sectors, with cotton and synthetics appearing as different sectors. Even if that level of disaggregation were empirically possible, perfect substitutability would still only be an approximation.

A formulation that allows aggregate commodity categories across countries but specifies product differentiation by country of origin into the structure of demand was proposed in a partial equilibrium setting by Armington (1969).[17] The structure is based on a two-level CES formulation which has been extremely useful in much of the empirical literature on estimating import

[15]Two-way trade has been observed in trade statistics even when products are classified in an extremely disaggregated form (Grubel & Lloyd, 1975).

[16]Empirical evidence by Isard (1978) indicates that for the most narrowly defined domestic and foreign goods, for which prices can be matched (four- and five-digit SITC categories), disparities among common currency prices of goods from different countries are systematically correlated with exchange rates rather than randomly fluctuating over time.

[17]The assumption of national product differentiation has often been referred to as the "Armington" assumption since Armington (1969) first investigated the nature of import demand functions when domestically produced and imported goods are imperfect substitutes.

demand functions (Leamer & Stern, 1970). It is also a very useful specification for building trade-oriented applied general equilibrium models for single economies (Dervis, De Melo & Robinson, 1982). The function has domestic and foreign goods that are combined, in a similar way to production inputs, to produce an aggregate output, and as a result the demands for domestic and foreign commodities are derived demands. This CES structure follows the form depicted in Equation 4.1.1, where C_i is the composite final demand, and C_i^m and C_i^d are the imported and domestic con-sumption goods respectively, and where A_i^c, δ_i^c and ρ_i^c are parameters.

$$C_i = \overline{A_i^c}\left[\delta_i^c C_i^{m^{-\rho_i^c}} + (1-\delta_i^c) C_i^{d^{-\rho_i^c}}\right]^{\frac{-1}{\rho_i^c}} \quad \text{where} \quad \rho_i^c < 1 \qquad (4.1.1)$$

The problem facing the buyer is to find a ratio of inputs (C_i^m and C_i^d) so that the marginal rate of substitution equals the ratio of the domestic and foreign goods prices. This is the condition for cost minimisation.

$$\frac{C_i^m}{C_i^d} = \left(\frac{\delta_i^c}{1-\delta_i^c}\right)^{\sigma_i^c}\left(\frac{P_i^d}{P_i^{cm}}\right)^{\sigma_i^c} \quad \text{where} \quad \sigma_i^c = \frac{1}{1+\rho_i^c} \qquad (4.1.2)$$

The magnitude of the trade substitution elasticity, and the import share determines how responsive domestic demand is to changes in the relative price of imported goods resulting from trade liberalisation. This treatment of international trade with the introduction of product differentiation adds greater flexibility to the description of how domestic sectors compete in the world economy.

There are many places further substitution could have been introduced, however most extensions require many more estimated parameters and further complicate the feedback mechanisms in the model, it is far from obvious that the gains offset the costs in a reasonably aggregated model.

The treatment of exports

The introduction of product differentiation will violate the small country assumption only if it is interpreted as requiring equality between domestic and world prices of tradables adjusted for tariffs. But if the small country assumption is taken to mean that the terms of trade of a country are fixed because the "dollar" prices of both its imports and exports are fixed, then this weaker form of the small country assumption need not be violated by introducing product differentiation and differences between the price of imports and exports, and domestically produced goods (Dervis, De Melo & Robinson, 1982).

On the import side, the small country assumption is merely a representation of the rest of the world's supply curves. Being small means constituting a small fraction of the market for goods produced in other countries, and as such the country cannot influence world prices. Product differentiation does not affect this type of smallness and the usual assumption of infinitely elastic foreign supply curves is appropriate. However, when it comes to maintaining the small country assumption on the export side, the situation is not so simple. When a country is selling a differentiated product, it may no longer be small in the market for that product. If we treat the rest of the world symmetrically with a single country, we must acknowledge that the demand for exports produced by a single country will be less than infinitely elastic. This implies that export prices are no longer fixed, and the small country assumption may no longer hold.

If the small country assumption were to hold, a country's export prices would be fixed in the world market, independent of the amount exported (as shown in Equation 4.1.3).

$$P_i^e = P_i^{we} ER \tag{4.1.3}$$

However in this case if $P_i^e > P_i^d$, no domestic sales would take place and all production would be exported. No domestic sales would take place until $P_i^e = P_i^d$ and so the domestic price would rise until it was at least $P_i^e = P_i^d$, so a situation with $P_i^e > P_i^d$ would never exist. In principle, it could occur if all domestic demands were sourced from imports, but since this is most unlikely, the only possibilities are $E_i > 0$ if $P_i^e = P_i^d$, and $E_i = 0$ if $P_i^e < P_i^d$. This treatment is faithful to the small country assumption, but is far from consistent with the assumption that products are differentiated by country of origin and imperfect substitutes for one another. The assumption of product differentiation naturally leads to less than infinitely elastic demand functions for a country's exports. These demand functions then take the general form seen in Equation 4.1.4 where Π_i is an "aggregate" world price for commodity i. Since the country is small, then Π_i can be assumed fixed, and now P_i^{we} is determined endogenously by domestic production costs and the exchange rate (as seen in Equation 4.1.5).

$$E_i = E_i(\Pi_i, P_i^{we}) \tag{4.1.4}$$

$$P_i^{we} = \frac{P_i^d}{ER} \tag{4.1.5}$$

A fall in P_i^{we}, with constant Π_i will now lead to an increase in demand for exports from sector i. Assuming the world as a whole behaves in a manner similar to the single country being modelled and consumes products according to the rules of cost minimisation subject to a generalised CES formulation that specifies composite world commodities, the world demand functions for a given country's product are of the following simple constant elasticity form, similar to a country's import demand functions.

$$E_i = \overline{E_i}\left(\frac{\Pi_i}{P_i^{we}}\right)^{\eta_i} \quad \text{where} \quad \eta_i > 0 \tag{4.1.6}$$

In Equation 4.1.6, η_i is the price elasticity of export demand, and $\overline{E_i}$ is a constant reflecting the initial level of exports by sector i when $\Pi_i = P_i^{we}$. Since the country is small, we can ignore changes in P_i^{we} on Π_i, but now a change in P_i^{we} can affect the country's market share in the world market. For example, if the price of New Zealand's agriculture exports were to rise, then the export market would not suddenly disappear, instead its market share would decline.

Modelling the environment

In order to model the effects of trade liberalisation on the environment, sectoral emissions are incorporated into the model. Each sector uses emissions as an intermediate good, in the form specified by the Leontief technology in the production function described by Equation 4.2.1 below. This amounts to a linear relationship between emissions and production. This relationship is detailed in Equation 4.1.7 where Z_i^x is the total production emissions of carbon dioxide by sector i, and ϕ_i^x is the rate at which output in sector i, X_i, produces carbon dioxide.

$$Z_i^x = \phi_i^x X_i \tag{4.1.7}$$

This assumption of Leontief technology does however limit the ways in which firms can respond to a ceiling on emissions, or a carbon tax. Firms are restricted to lowering output in order to lower their emissions, they cannot substitute between inputs with different emission rates, nor can they utilise less polluting technology.

In addition to emissions being incorporated as an intermediate good in production, the consumption of goods is also treated as generating emissions. This relationship is analogous to that above for production and is detailed in Equation 4.1.8, where Z_i^c is the consumption emissions of carbon dioxide by sector i, and ϕ_i^c is the rate at which consumption of sector i, C_i, produces carbon dioxide.

$$Z_i^c = \phi_i^c C_i \tag{4.1.8}$$

Thus, the total emissions attributable to each sector from both production and consumption can be seen in Equation 4.1.9.

$$Z_i = Z_i^x + Z_i^c \tag{4.1.9}$$

In case two of the scenarios to be modelled, the aggregate level of economy-wide emissions (shown in Equation 4.1.10) is required to meet the condition represented in Equation 4.1.11. This is in effect, what is required by the FCCC whereby carbon dioxide emissions must not exceed the level that existed in 1990. In order to enforce this condition in the model it is desirable to include an endogenous emissions tax, as seen in the last term in Equations 4.1.12 and 4.1.13. This requires the price of both domestic production and consumption goods to include the cost of that goods contribution to economy-wide emissions, so that the most polluting goods have to pay the highest tax. This has the effect that consumers will react by substituting away from these higher priced goods, and so their production and/or consumption will fall along with their contribution to emissions.

$$Z = \sum_{i=1}^{n} Z_i \tag{4.1.10}$$

$$Z \leq \overline{Z_{1990}} \tag{4.1.11}$$

$$P_i^d X_i = X_i \frac{1}{A_i^x} \left[\delta_i^{x\sigma_i^x} R^{(1-\sigma_i^x)} + (1-\delta_i^x)^{\sigma_i^x} W^{(1-\sigma_i^x)} \right]^{\frac{1}{(1-\sigma_i^x)}} + \sum_{j=1}^{n} \alpha_{ji} X_i P_{ji}^n + \phi_i^x X_i t^z \tag{4.1.12}$$

$$P_i^c = \frac{1}{A_i^c} \left[\delta_i^{c\sigma_i^c} P_i^{cm(1-\sigma_i^c)} + (1-\delta_i^c)^{\sigma_i^c} P_i^{d(1-\sigma_i^c)} \right]^{\frac{1}{(1-\sigma_i^c)}} + \phi_i^c t^z \tag{4.1.13}$$

Model equations

The complete set of equations describing the model is given in Table 4.1. Definitions of endogenous variables, exogenous variables and parameters are given in Tables 4.2 and 4.3, respectively. Variable subscripts indicate sectors, of which there are $i, j = 1, \ldots, n$. If double subscripts are employed, the first subscript denotes the sector of origin while the second denotes the sector of destination. Uppercase letters are reserved for endogenous variables, unless they have a bar, in which case they are exogenous or normalisation constants. Parameters are denoted by Greek letters. The exception to these rules is the emissions tax t^z, which is endogenous.

Production is characterised by two-level nesting (see Figure 4.1(a) above). At the first level is a Leontief input-output production function

Table 4.1 Multisectoral CGE Model Equations.

Objective Function

Maximise utility/welfare function

$$\max U = \prod_{i=1}^{n} (C_i - \gamma_i^c)^{\beta_i} \quad \text{where} \quad \sum_{i=1}^{n} \beta_i = 1, \beta_i > 0 \qquad (1) \qquad (4.2.15)$$

Production

Production function

$$X_i = \overline{A_i^x} \left[\delta_i^x K_i^{-\rho_i^x} + (1 - \delta_i^x) L_i^{-\rho_i^x} \right]^{\frac{-1}{\rho_i^x}} \qquad (2) \qquad (4.2.2)$$

Factor Markets

Labour demand

$$W = \left(\frac{(1 - \delta_i^x)}{\overline{A_i^x}^{\rho_i^x}} X_i^{1+\rho_i^x} L_i^{-(1+\rho_i^x)} \right) P_i^v \qquad (3) \qquad (4.2.3)$$

Capital demand

$$R = \left(\frac{\delta_i^x}{\overline{A_i^x}^{\rho_i^x}} X_i^{1+\rho_i^x} L_i^{-(1+\rho_i^x)} \right) P_i^v \qquad (4) \qquad (4.2.4)$$

Labour supply (labour market equilibrium)

$$\sum_{i=1}^{n} L_i = \overline{L} \qquad (5) \qquad (4.2.5)$$

Capital supply (capital market equilibrium)

$$\sum_{i=1}^{n} K_i = \overline{K} \qquad (6) \qquad (4.2.6)$$

Intermediate Products Demand

Demand for domestic intermediates by sector i from sector j

$$N_{ji}^d = \alpha_{ji}^d X_i \qquad (7) \qquad (4.2.7)$$

Table 4.1 Multisectoral CGE Model Equations (continued).

Demand for foreign intermediates by sector i from sector j

$$N_{ji}^{m} = \alpha_{ji}^{m} X_i \qquad (8) \qquad (4.2.8)$$

Output Allocation for Tradables

$$X_i = D_i + E_i \qquad (9) \qquad (4.2.9)$$

Prices

Value-added price

$$P_i^{v} = P_i^{d} - \sum_{i=1}^{n} \alpha_{ji}^{d} P_j^{d} - \sum_{j=1}^{n} \alpha_{ji}^{m} P_j^{nm} - \phi_i^{x} t^{z} \qquad (10) \qquad (4.2.10)$$

Composite consumption price

$$P_i^{c} = \frac{1}{A_i^{c}} \left[\delta_i^{c\,\sigma_i^c} P_i^{cm\,(1-\sigma_i^c)} + (1-\delta_i^c)^{\sigma_i^c} P_i^{d\,(1-\sigma_i^c)} \right]^{\frac{1}{(1-\sigma_i^c)}} + \phi_i^c t^z \qquad (11) \qquad (4.2.20)$$

Definition of Internal Prices of Traded Goods

Import prices

$$P_i^{nm} = (1 + t_i^{nm}) \overline{P_i^{wnm}} \, ER \qquad (12) \qquad (4.2.11)$$

$$P_i^{cm} = (1 + t_i^{cm}) \overline{P_i^{wcm}} \, ER \qquad (13) \qquad (4.2.12)$$

Export price

$$P_i^{we} = \frac{P_i^{d}}{ER} \qquad (14) \qquad (4.2.13)$$

Import Supply and Export Demand

Export demand

$$E_i = \overline{E_i} \left(\frac{\Pi_i}{P_i^{we}} \right)^{\eta_{ij}}, \quad \text{where} \quad \eta_i > 0 \qquad (15) \qquad (4.2.14)$$

Table 4.1 Multisectoral CGE Model Equations (continued).

Consumer and Intermediate Demand

Consumer demand

$$C_i = \gamma_i^c + \beta_i \left(\frac{Y - \sum_{j=1}^{n} P_j^c \gamma_j^c}{P_i^c} \right) \qquad (16) \quad (4.2.17)$$

CES composite consumption

$$C_i = \overline{A_i^c} \left[\delta_i^c {C_i^m}^{-\rho_i^c} + (1-\delta_i^c) {C_i^d}^{-\rho_i^c} \right]^{\frac{-1}{\rho_i^c}} \quad \text{where} \quad \rho_i^c < 1 \qquad (17) \quad (4.2.18)$$

Cost-minimising choice of consumption from domestic and foreign sources

$$\frac{C_i^m}{C_i^d} = \left(\frac{\delta_i^c}{1-\delta_i^c} \right)^{\sigma_i^c} \left(\frac{P_i^d}{P_i^{cm}} \right)^{\sigma_i^c} \quad \text{where} \quad \sigma_i^c = \frac{1}{1+\rho_i^c} \qquad (18) \quad (4.2.19)$$

Domestic intermediate demand

$$N_i^d = \sum_{j=1}^{n} N_{ij}^d \qquad (19) \quad (4.2.21)$$

Imported intermediate demand

$$N_i^m = \sum_{j=1}^{n} N_{ij}^m \qquad (20) \quad (2.2.22)$$

Total domestic demand

$$D_i = N_i^d + C_i^d \qquad (21) \quad (4.2.23)$$

Emissions

Sectoral production emissions

$$Z_i^x = \phi_i^x X_i \qquad (22) \quad (4.2.24)$$

Sectoral consumption emissions

$$Z_i^c = \phi_i^c C_i \qquad (23) \quad (4.2.25)$$

Table 4.1 Multisectoral CGE Model Equations (continued).

Total sectoral emissions

$$Z_i = Z_i^x + Z_i^c \qquad (24) \quad (4.2.26)$$

Total economy-wide emissions

$$Z = \sum_{i=1}^{n} Z_i \qquad (25) \quad (4.2.27)$$

FCCC constraint

$$Z \leq \overline{Z_{1990}} \qquad (26) \quad (4.2.28)$$

Government Revenue, Trade Balance and Income Definition

Income

$$Y = \sum_{i=1}^{n} (W_i L_i + R_i K_i) + G + ER\,\overline{B} \qquad (27) \quad (4.2.29)$$

Tariff revenue

$$Tm = \sum_{i=1}^{n} \left(P_i^{nm} - \frac{P_i^{nm}}{(1+t_i^{nm})} \right) N_i^m + \sum_{i=1}^{n} \left(P_i^{cm} - \frac{P_i^{cm}}{(1+t_i^{cm})} \right) C_i^m \qquad (28) \quad (4.2.30)$$

Emission tax revenue

$$Tz = \sum_{i=1}^{n} t^z Z_i \qquad (29) \quad (4.2.31)$$

Government revenue

$$G = Tm + Tz \qquad (30) \quad (4.2.32)$$

Trade balance constraint

$$\sum_{i=1}^{n} \left(\overline{P_i^{wnm}}\, N_i^m + \overline{P_i^{wcm}}\, C_i^m - P_i^{we} E_i \right) = \overline{B} \qquad (31) \quad (4.2.33)$$

Table 4.1 Multisectoral CGE Model Equations (continued).

Market Equilibrium

Zero profit condition

$$P_i^d X_i = \frac{1}{A_i^x}\left[\delta_i^{x^{\sigma_i^x}} R^{(1-\sigma_i^x)} + (1-\delta_i^x)^{\sigma_i^x} W^{(1-\sigma_i^x)}\right]^{\frac{1}{(1-\sigma_i^x)}} + \sum_{j=1}^{n} \alpha_{ji}^d X_i P_j^d + \sum_{j=1}^{n} \alpha_{ji}^m X_i P_j^{nm} + \phi_i^x X_i t^z \qquad (32) \quad (4.2.34)$$

Numeraire

Constant domestic price level

$$1 = \frac{\sum_{j=1}^{n} P_j^d D_j^0}{\sum_{j=1}^{n} P_j^{d0} D_j^0} \qquad (33) \quad (4.2.35)$$

(Equation 4.2.1). At this level, firms use a composite of primary factors of production, emissions and *n* composite intermediate inputs, one for each sector. Since the composite primary factor cannot be substituted for the composite intermediate or emissions, nor can intermediates of one sector be substituted for intermediates of another, the production function at level one is strongly separable (Blackorby, Primont & Russel, 1978 or Phillips, 1974). At the second level each of the composite functions is defined. The primary factor of production is a composite of two primary factors — capital and labour. Primary factors of production substitute smoothly for each other through CES value-added functions given in Equation 4.2.2. The parameters of the CES vary across sectors. Each sector uses intermediate inputs, where these inputs come from both domestic and foreign sources. Intermediate inputs from a given sector, are sourced from domestic and foreign intermediate inputs. Firms do not substitute between domestic and foreign intermediate inputs in a given sector and as such they enter production with fixed coefficients (Leontief technology) as seen in Equations 4.2.7 and 4.2.8. Emissions also enter into each sector's production in the form of a non-traded intermediate input.

Table 4.2 Endogenous Variables.

U	Utility
C_i	Composite final consumption of sector i
X_i	Gross output of sector i
K_i	Sectoral capital stocks
L_i	Sectoral employment
W	Economy-wide wage rate
R	Economy-wide rental rate
N_{ji}^d	Domestic intermediate purchases of sector i from sector j
N_{ji}^m	Imported intermediate purchases of sector i from sector j
D_i	Supply for domestic sales
E_i	Supply for export sales
P_i^v	Value-added price of sector i
P_i^d	Unit price of domestically sold goods
P_i^c	Unit price of composite consumption of sector i
P_i^{nm}	Price of intermediate imports of sector i
P_i^{cm}	Price of consumption imports of sector i
P_i^{we}	World price of exports from sector i
Y	Disposable income
C_i^d	Consumer demand for domestic goods
C_i^m	Consumer demand for imported goods
N_i^d	Intermediate demand for domestic goods
N_i^m	Intermediate demand for imported goods
Z_i^x	Production emissions of sector i
Z_i^c	Consumption emissions of sector i
Z_i	Carbon dioxide emissions of sector i
Z	Total carbon dioxide emissions
G	Government revenue
ER	Exchange rate
Tm	Tariff revenue
Tz	Carbon tax revenue
t^z	Carbon tax rate

Table 4.3 Exogenous Variables and Parameters.

Exogenous Variables	
$\overline{L}$	Labour supply
$\overline{K}$	Capital supply
t_i^{nm}	Tariff rate on sector *i* intermediate imports
t_i^{cm}	Tariff rate on sector *i* consumption imports
$\overline{P_i^{wnm}}$	World price of intermediate imports
$\overline{P_i^{wcm}}$	World price of consumption imports
$\overline{P_i^{we}}$	World price of exports
$\overline{E_i}$	Initial level of exports
Π_i	Average world price of exports
$\overline{Z_{1990}}$	1990 carbon dioxide emissions level
$\overline{B}$	Exogenous component of the current account in foreign dollars
Parameters	
$\overline{A_i^x}, \overline{A_i^c}$	Normalisation constants (see Appendix A)
γ_i^c, β_i	Parameters of the linear expenditure system
δ_i^x, δ_i^c	Quasi-share parameters of various CES functions
σ_i^x, σ_i^c	Elasticities of substitution in final and intermediate demand
ρ_i^x, ρ_i^c	Parameters corresponding to the elasticities (in particular $\sigma = \frac{1}{1+\rho}$)
η_i	Export elasticity
α_{ji}^d	Ratio of domestic intermediate *j* used in the production of *i*
α_{ji}^m	Ratio of foreign intermediate *j* used in the production of *i*
ϕ_i^x	Propensity for production to emit carbon dioxide in sector *i*
ϕ_i^c	Propensity for consumption to emit carbon dioxide in sector *i*

These assumptions are reflected in the first level Leontief production function:

$$X_i = \min\left[F_1(K_i, L_i), \frac{N_{1i}}{\alpha_{1i}}, \ldots, \frac{N_{ni}}{\alpha_{ni}}, \frac{Z_i}{\phi_i} \right], \tag{4.2.1}$$

where X_i is the gross output of sector i. The functions $F_1(K_i, L_i)$ are the CES value-added functions in labour and capital.

The production function in Equation 4.2.2 is the result of profit maximisation by the representative firm with respect to its variable inputs, capital, labour, emissions and intermediates, subject to the technology description in the above equation.

$$X_i = \overline{A_i^x}\left[\delta_i^x K_i^{-\rho_i^x} + (1 - \delta_i^x) L_i^{-\rho_i^x} \right]^{\frac{-1}{\rho_i^x}} \tag{4.2.2}$$

Factor demands are given by Equations 4.2.3 and 4.2.4, where the factor prices (the marginal products) are obtained by taking partial derivatives of the production function with respect to the relevant factor.

$$W = \left(\frac{(1 - \delta_i^x)}{\overline{A_i^x}^{\rho_i^x}} X_i^{1+\rho_i^x} L_i^{-(1+\rho_i^x)} \right) P_i^v \tag{4.2.3}$$

$$R = \left(\frac{\delta_i^x}{\overline{A_i^x}^{\rho_i^x}} X_i^{1+\rho_i^x} L_i^{-(1+\rho_i^x)} \right) P_i^v \tag{4.2.4}$$

It is assumed that factor endowments are fixed, and this is reflected in Equations 4.2.5 and 4.2.6.

$$\sum_{i=1}^{n} L_i = \overline{L} \tag{4.2.5}$$

$$\sum_{i=1}^{n} K_i = \overline{K} \tag{4.2.6}$$

Equations 4.2.7 and 4.2.8 describe the demand for domestically and foreign produced intermediates. Equation 4.2.7 describes the demand for domestically sourced intermediate purchases in sector i from sector j resulting from the Leontief technology assumption in Equation 4.2.1, where α_{ij}^{d} and α_{ji}^{m} are the ratios of domestic and foreign intermediate j used in the production of i respectively. In turn, Equation 4.2.8 describes the demand for foreign-sourced intermediate purchases in sector i from sector j.

$$N_{ji}^{d} = \alpha_{ji}^{d} X_i \qquad (4.2.7)$$

$$N_{ji}^{m} = \alpha_{ji}^{m} X_i \qquad (4.2.8)$$

Equation 4.2.9 describes the output allocation of tradables where the excess of domestic production over domestic demand is exported.

$$X_i = D_i + E_i \qquad (4.2.9)$$

Equation 4.2.10 is the value-added price, or net price per unit of output.

$$P_i^{v} = P_i^{d} - \sum_{j=1}^{n} \alpha_{ji}^{d} P_j^{d} - \sum_{j=1}^{n} \alpha_{ji}^{m} P_j^{nm} - \phi_i^{x} t^{z} \qquad (4.2.10)$$

The relationship between border or world prices and internal prices is given in Equations 4.2.11 to 4.2.13. Since there is no money metric in the model, all prices are relative prices defined in terms of the selected numeraire. In Equation 4.2.12, P_i^{cm} is the number of units of the numeraire good that consumers must pay for one unit of the import variety of sector i, and $\overline{P_i^{wcm}}$ is the border or world price of the same good relative to the numeraire. The exchange rate variable, ER, converts the world price of goods in any sector into the price paid by consumers exclusive of tariffs. Equation 4.2.13 shows the relationship between export prices and domestic production costs.

$$P_i^{nm} = (1 + t_i^{nm})\overline{P_i^{wnm}}\, ER \qquad (4.2.11)$$

$$P_i^{cm} = (1 + t_i^{cm})\overline{P_i^{wcm}}\, ER \tag{4.2.12}$$

$$P_i^{we} = \frac{P_i^d}{ER} \tag{4.2.13}$$

Equation 4.2.14 defines the extent of monopsony power New Zealand has on world markets. It is assumed that New Zealand has no monopoly power with respect to imports, and has significant monopsony power only in agricultural products. This is reflected in the size of the export elasticity term (η_i) in Equation 4.2.14.

$$E_i = \overline{E_i}\left(\frac{\Pi_i}{P_i^{we}}\right)^{\eta_i} \quad \text{where} \quad \eta_i > 0 \tag{4.2.14}$$

Equations 4.2.15 through to 4.2.19 describe consumer demand. The consumer maximises the Stone-Geary utility function in Equation 4.2.15 of all final commodities (both imported and domestic) subject to consumer income given by Equation 4.2.16. We assume that the imported and domestic commodities in a given sector substitute in the consumers' utility function in a CES nest given by Equation 4.2.18. This implies that the top level Stone-Geary utility function is weakly separable in the composite final commodities of the model. Moreover because the commodity aggregator is linearly homogeneous, the price index of the composite commodity can be represented by the unit cost function (Equation 4.2.20) that is dual to the commodity aggregator (Equation 4.2.18). Weak separability combined with the existence of the price index of composite commodities implies that the consumers decision problem may be decomposed into "two-stage budgeting".[18] Thus in the first stage (or top level) the consumer maximises the separable Stone-Geary utility function of composite commodities, given income and composite prices. This results in a consumer demand function of the form seen in Equation 4.2.17.

[18]De Melo and Tarr (1992).

$$\max U = \prod_{i=1}^{n} (C_i - \gamma_i^c)^{\beta_i} \quad \text{where} \quad \sum_{i=1}^{n} \beta_i \equiv 1, \; \beta_i > 0 \tag{4.2.15}$$

$$\text{subject to} \quad Y = \sum_{i=1}^{n} P_i^c C_i \tag{4.2.16}$$

$$\Rightarrow \quad C_i = \gamma_i^c + \beta_i \left(\frac{Y - \sum_{j=1}^{n} P_j^c \gamma_j^c}{P_i^c} \right) \tag{4.2.17}$$

In the second stage, the consumer maximises each of the subutility functions (Equation 4.2.18) subject to expenditure allocated to consumption of the *i*th commodity from the first stage maximisation.

$$C_i = \overline{A_i^c} \left[\delta_i^c C_i^{m^{-\rho_i^c}} + (1 - \delta_i^c) C_i^{d^{-\rho_i^c}} \right]^{\frac{-1}{\rho_i^c}} \quad \text{where} \quad \rho_i^c < 1 \tag{4.2.18}$$

Equations 4.2.18 and 4.2.19 describe the choice between domestic and foreign produced consumption goods. Equation 4.2.19 describes the cost-minimising choice of domestic and foreign purchases from sector *i*, subject to the constraint that substitution possibilities between domestic and imported consumption goods are characterised by Equation 4.2.18. The consumers cost minimising choice of domestic and imported consumer goods is depicted in Figure 4.2.

$$\frac{C_i^m}{C_i^d} = \left(\frac{\delta_i^c}{1 - \delta_i^c} \right)^{\sigma_i^c} \left(\frac{P_i^d}{P_i^{cm}} \right)^{\sigma_i^c} \quad \text{where} \quad \sigma_i^c = \frac{1}{1 + \rho_i^c} \tag{4.2.19}$$

Equation 4.2.20 defines the price index of the composite consumption good. Here, the price index is dual to the corresponding unit quantity aggregator function. For example Equation 4.2.20 is the unit cost function that is dual to Equation 4.2.18, with $C_i = 1$. Since the quantity aggregator function (Equation 4.2.21) is linearly homogeneous, the total costs of C_i may be written as $P_i^c C_i$ where P_i^c is the unit cost function (Equation 4.2.20)

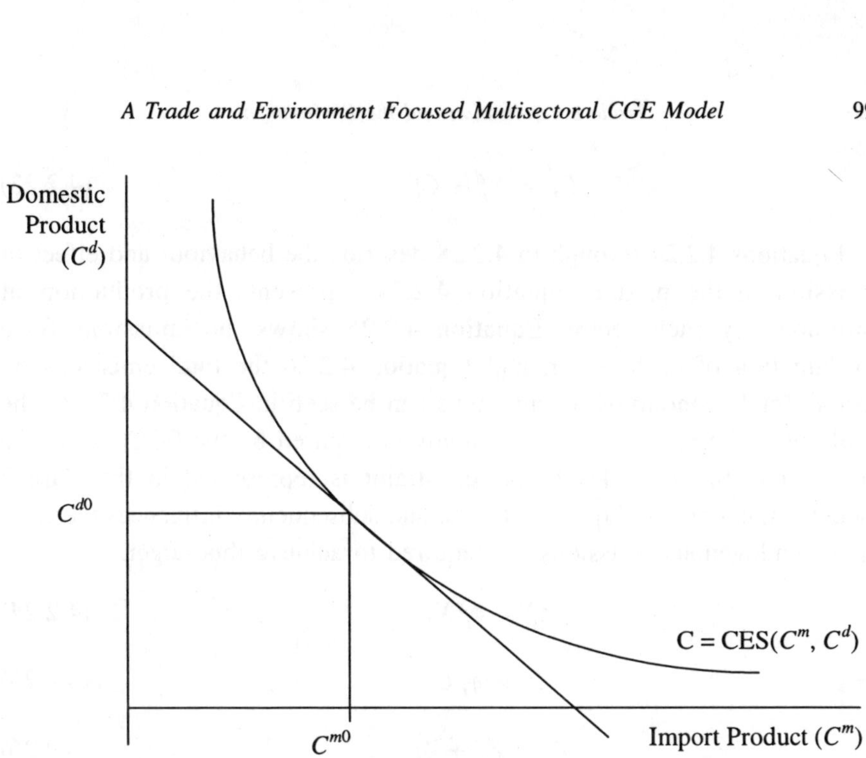

Figure 4.2 The Elasticity of Substitution and Cost Minimisation in Consumption Demand.

(Varian, 1984). This implies that the average cost of C_i, when purchased at minimum cost, is independent of the number of units purchased, so the unit cost function is an acceptable price index.

$$P_i^c = \frac{1}{A_i^c}\left[\delta_i^{c\,\sigma_i^c} P_i^{cm\,(1-\sigma_i^c)} + (1-\delta_i^c)^{\sigma_i^c} P_i^{d\,(1-\sigma_i^c)} \right]^{\frac{1}{(1-\sigma_i^c)}} + \phi_i^c t^z \qquad (4.2.20)$$

Equation 4.2.21 represents the total demand for domestic intermediates from sector i, and similarly for imported intermediates in Equation 4.2.22. Total domestic demand for sector i is represented in Equation 4.2.23.

$$N_i^d = \sum_{j=1}^{n} N_{ij}^d \qquad (4.2.21)$$

$$N_i^m = \sum_{j=1}^{n} N_{ij}^m \qquad (4.2.22)$$

$$D_i = N_i^d + C_i^d \tag{4.2.23}$$

Equations 4.2.24 through to 4.2.28 describe the behaviour and effect of emission in the model. Equation 4.2.24 represents the production of emissions by each sector, Equation 4.2.25 shows the emissions from consumption of each sector, and Equation 4.2.26 the total emissions by sector. Total economy-wide emissions can be seen in Equation 4.2.27. The total level of emissions in the economy is required by the FCCC to be no higher than the 1990 level, this constraint is represented in the Case 2 model simulations by Equation 4.2.28, and subsequently influences the level of the endogenous emissions tax required to achieve this target.

$$Z_i^x = \phi_i^x X_i \tag{4.2.24}$$

$$Z_i^c = \phi_i^c C_i \tag{4.2.25}$$

$$Z_i = Z_i^x + Z_i^c \tag{4.2.26}$$

$$Z = \sum_{i=1}^{n} Z_i \tag{4.2.27}$$

$$Z \leq \overline{Z_{1990}} \tag{4.2.28}$$

Equation 4.2.29 is the income expenditure identity, which states that the consumer's income derives from factor income and government lump sum distributions, less the current account deficit. Given that all agents in the model (firms, consumers and government) satisfy a budget constraint, it is well-known that the sum of the excess demands for all goods is zero, and therefore Walras' law holds.

$$Y = \sum_{i=1}^{n} (W_i L_i + R_i K_i) + G + ER\overline{B} \tag{4.2.29}$$

Total tariff revenue and emissions tax revenue, are detailed in Equations 4.2.30 and 4.2.31, where the sum of these two make up total government revenue as shown in Equation 4.2.32.

$$Tm = \sum_{i=1}^{n}\left(P_i^{nm} - \frac{P_i^{nm}}{(1+t_i^{nm})}\right)N_i^m + \sum_{i=1}^{n}\left(P_i^{cm} - \frac{P_i^{cm}}{(1+t_i^{cm})}\right)C_i^m \quad (4.2.30)$$

$$Tz = \sum_{i=1}^{n} t^z Z_i \quad (4.2.31)$$

$$G = Tm + Tz \quad (4.2.32)$$

The model includes a current account constraint in Equation 4.2.33 so that trade policy changes are not financed by a free lunch from the rest of the world. That is, without a balance of trade constraint, import liberalisation, which results in increased imports in the liberalising sector, is not required to be offset by increased exports or decreased imports elsewhere. This is an unrealistic assumption, which implies a permanent increase in capital inflow from the rest of the world. De Melo & Tarr (1992) show that this misspecification can lead to a severe over-estimate of the benefits of trade liberalisation. The trade deficit prevailing in the base year is thus unaffected by changes in trade policy. Moreover, the current account constraint is expressed in foreign units because otherwise the balance of trade would be variable.

$$\sum_{i}^{n}\left(\overline{P_i^{wnm}}\, N_i^m + \overline{P_i^{wcm}}\, C_i^m - P_i^{we} E_i\right) = \overline{B} \quad (4.2.33)$$

Prices are determined by a zero profit condition in Equation 4.2.34, and this also represents market equilibrium.

$$P_i^d X_i = X_i \frac{1}{A_i^x}\left[\delta_i^{x\,\sigma_i^x} R^{(1-\sigma_i^x)} + (1-\delta_i^x)^{\sigma_i^x} W^{(1-\sigma_i^x)}\right]^{\frac{1}{(1-\sigma_i^x)}}$$
$$+ \sum_{j=1}^{n} \alpha_{ji}^d X_i P_{ji}^d + \sum_{j=1}^{n} \alpha_{ji}^m X_i P_{ji}^{nm} + \phi_i^x X_i t^z \quad (4.2.34)$$

The entire system of equations is homogeneous of degree zero in prices, i.e. a proportionate change in all prices does not change any demand or supply function. Since this implies that only relative prices matter, it is necessary to choose a numeraire to determine prices and to close the model. A convenient numeraire for this purpose is a weighted average of all domestic prices (Equation 4.2.35).

$$1 = \frac{\sum_{j=1}^{n} P_j^d D_j^0}{\sum_{j=1}^{n} P_j^{d0} D_j^0} \tag{4.2.35}$$

— Chapter 5 —

Simulation Results from the Multisectoral CGE Model

Introduction

Within the trade and environment literature there is a general consensus that trade policies are a poor substitute for domestic environmental policies, and that trade liberalisation and environmental protection can be treated as separate objectives.[1] However there has been very little attention paid to the empirical or computable quantification of these results.

The objective of this study is to attempt to assess the magnitude of the effects of trade liberalisation on welfare and emissions levels, and the degree to which these effects are influenced by environmental policy. These effects are analysed within the New Zealand economy, however the results that follow are widely applicable to other small open market-based economies. The results of this study will assist in providing direction for New Zealand's trade and environmental policies and should help to fill some of the empirical vacuum in this field. It is expected based on theoretical analyses in the literature, that the results will show trade liberalisation to be welfare-enhancing, and for it to have a minimal impact on environmental quality, in the presence of environmental policies that internalise environmental externalities.

Because the questions raised in this study have economy-wide implications, this study has employed a computable general equilibrium (CGE) model for the New Zealand economy, incorporating a trade and environment focus

[1]See for example Bhagwati (1981).

to assess the consequences of trade and environmental policies. By specifically including the environment (in the form of emissions), it will be possible to achieve a detailed and precise analysis of trade liberalisation's environmental effects in New Zealand, and whether it remains a welfare-enhancing policy change. This analysis is performed both with and without an emissions tax to evaluate trade liberalisation and environmental degradation scenarios. These questions are easily examined in a general equilibrium context and the results of the two policies, not only on the environment, but also on the rest of the economy, can be compared. Furthermore, only a general equilibrium evaluation of these policies can assess the impacts of their respective effects on welfare.

This chapter presents the results and analysis of the policy scenario simulations on emissions, welfare and the economy as a whole. The policy scenarios are then compared and analysed, and are followed by a summary of the results.

Simulation Results and Analysis

In this section the results of the policy simulations are presented and analysed. In order to assess the effects of trade liberalisation and environmental policy on emissions levels and welfare, two policy scenarios are simulated. These are:

Case 1 — The effects of trade liberalisation are examined in the absence of a carbon tax.

Case 2 — The effects of trade liberalisation are examined in the presence of a carbon tax.

The simulation results from these two policy scenarios are then compared and their respective effects analysed.

Case 1: The effects of trade liberalisation in the absence of a carbon tax

The investigation of the effects of trade liberalisation, in the absence of a carbon tax, on emissions and welfare within the CGE model presented in this study is a relatively simple process. Following calibration and benchmarking of the model to the initial equilibrium (see Appendix A), trade liberalisation can be simulated simply by implementing the model with all tariffs set to zero and generating the new equilibrium.

The projected effects of both policy simulations are listed in Table 5.1. The first column of the table contains the endogenous variables values in the initial equilibrium before the policy simulations. The second column shows the values the endogenous variables take on in the new equilibrium following the simulation of Case 1. Similarly the values of endogenous variables in the new equilibrium following the simulation of Case 2 are presented in column 3. Column 4 contains the percentage change in the endogenous variables between the initial equilibrium and the policy simulation in Case 1. The percentage changes in the endogenous variables between the policy simulation of Cases 1 and 2 can be seen in column 5. Finally, in column 6, the percentage change in the endogenous variables between the initial equilibrium and the policy simulation of Case 2 is presented. In the presentation of the effects of trade liberalisation in the absence of a carbon tax, columns 1, 2 and 4 are examined. Then by using the results presented in columns 2, 3, 5 and 6, the effects of trade liberalisation in the presence of a carbon tax are examined. Finally, when comparing the policy scenario simulations all columns will be considered.

The overall effects on the economy of trade liberalisation in the absence of a carbon tax are reported first, this is then followed by a presentation of the specific effects on emissions and welfare.

Overall effects on the economy

As can be seen in Table 5.1, trade liberalisation leads to a fall in the price of imported intermediate and consumption goods, with the largest falls occurring in the sectors exhibiting the highest tariffs. The price of agricultural imports falls by 3.3 per cent, textile imports by 16.3 per cent, chemical imports by 7.5 per cent, manufacturing imports by 7.7 per cent and service imports by 1.1 per cent. This fall in the prices of imports results in the prices of composite consumption goods also falling albeit to a lesser degree.

Table 5.1 Policy Scenario Simulation Results.

Variable	i j	Value			Per Cent Change		
		Case 0 (Initial)	Case 1	Case 2	Case 0 ⇒ 1	Case 1 ⇒ 2	Case 0 ⇒ 2
Utility		1.318	1.326	1.326	0.6%	0.0%	0.6%
Production	AGF	2.236	2.352	2.316	5.2%	−1.5%	3.6%
	TEX	0.275	1.036	0.942	276.7%	−9.1%	242.5%
	CHE	0.418	0.491	0.706	17.5%	43.8%	68.9%
	MAN	2.449	2.468	2.209	0.8%	−10.5%	−9.8%
	SER	8.369	7.821	7.952	−6.5%	1.7%	−5.0%
Capital	AGF	0.309	0.329	0.327	6.5%	−0.6%	5.8%
	TEX	0.012	0.045	0.041	275.0%	−8.9%	241.7%
	CHE	0.072	0.086	0.124	19.4%	44.2%	72.2%
	MAN	0.629	0.638	0.573	1.4%	−10.2%	−8.9%
	SER	1.392	1.316	1.349	−5.5%	2.5%	−3.1%
Labour	AGF	0.477	0.498	0.488	4.4%	−2.0%	2.3%
	TEX	0.054	0.202	0.184	274.1%	−8.9%	240.7%
	CHE	0.066	0.076	0.109	15.2%	43.4%	65.2%
	MAN	0.293	0.292	0.259	−0.3%	−11.3%	−11.6%
	SER	2.490	2.312	2.340	−7.1%	1.2%	−6.0%
Wage Rate		1.000	1.027	1.017	2.7%	−1.0%	1.7%
Rental Rate		1.000	0.989	0.956	−1.1%	−3.3%	−4.4%
Value-Added Price	AGF	0.352	0.356	0.349	1.1%	−2.0%	−0.9%
	TEX	0.239	0.243	0.240	1.7%	−1.2%	0.4%
	CHE	0.331	0.333	0.325	0.6%	−2.4%	−1.8%
	MAN	0.377	0.377	0.367	0.0%	−2.7%	−2.7%
	SER	0.464	0.470	0.462	1.3%	−1.7%	−0.4%
Unit Domestic Price	AGF	1.000	1.003	1.008	0.3%	0.5%	0.8%
	TEX	1.000	0.980	0.985	−2.0%	0.5%	−1.5%
	CHE	1.000	0.984	0.984	−1.6%	0.0%	−1.6%
	MAN	1.000	0.988	0.998	−1.2%	1.0%	−0.2%
	SER	1.000	1.004	1.000	0.4%	−0.4%	0.0%
Composite Final Consumption	AGF	0.377	0.377	0.377	0.0%	0.0%	0.0%
	TEX	0.128	0.136	0.136	6.3%	0.0%	6.3%
	CHE	0.175	0.180	0.172	2.9%	−4.4%	−1.7%
	MAN	1.038	1.052	1.048	1.3%	−0.4%	1.0%
	SER	3.848	3.842	3.853	−0.2%	0.3%	0.1%

Table 5.1 Policy Scenario Simulation Results (continued).

Variable	*i*	*j*	Value			Per Cent Change		
			Case 0 (Initial)	Case 1	Case 2	Case 0 ⇒ 1	Case 1 ⇒ 2	Case 0 ⇒ 2
Consumer	AGF		0.321	0.319	0.319	−0.6%	0.0%	−0.6%
Demand for	TEX		0.071	0.062	0.062	−12.7%	0.0%	−12.7%
Domestic	CHE		0.085	0.082	0.079	−3.5%	−3.7%	−7.1%
Produced	MAN		0.888	0.882	0.877	−0.7%	−0.6%	−1.2%
Goods	SER		3.658	3.647	3.660	−0.3%	0.4%	0.1%
Consumer	AGF		0.055	0.058	0.058	5.5%	0.0%	5.5%
Demand for	TEX		0.058	0.075	0.075	29.3%	0.0%	29.3%
Foreign	CHE		0.090	0.098	0.093	8.9%	−5.1%	3.3%
Produced	MAN		0.150	0.171	0.172	14.0%	0.6%	14.7%
Goods	SER		0.190	0.195	0.193	2.6%	−1.0%	1.6%
Unit Price of	AGF		1.000	0.997	1.006	−0.3%	0.9%	0.6%
Composite	TEX		1.000	0.908	0.917	−9.2%	1.0%	−8.3%
Consumption	CHE		1.000	0.953	1.040	−4.7%	9.1%	4.0%
	MAN		1.000	0.978	0.991	−2.2%	1.3%	−0.9%
	SER		1.000	1.003	1.004	0.3%	0.1%	0.4%
Price of	AGF		1.000	0.967	0.971	−3.3%	0.4%	−2.9%
Consumption	TEX		1.000	0.837	0.841	−16.3%	0.5%	−15.9%
Imports	CHE		1.000	0.925	0.929	−7.5%	0.4%	−7.1%
	MAN		1.000	0.923	0.927	−7.7%	0.4%	−7.3%
	SER		1.000	0.989	0.994	−1.1%	0.5%	−0.6%
Intermediate	AGF		1.112	1.336	1.302	20.1%	−2.5%	17.1%
Demand for	TEX		0.086	0.194	0.180	125.6%	−7.2%	109.3%
Domestic	CHE		0.290	0.305	0.325	5.2%	6.6%	12.1%
Produced	MAN		1.231	1.215	1.197	−1.3%	−1.5%	−2.8%
Goods	SER		4.174	4.147	4.151	−0.6%	0.1%	−0.6%
Intermediate	AGF		0.048	0.055	0.054	14.6%	−1.8%	12.5%
Demand for	TEX		0.058	0.158	0.145	172.4%	−8.2%	150.0%
Foreign	CHE		0.251	0.273	0.308	8.8%	12.8%	22.7%
Produced	MAN		0.422	0.419	0.396	−0.7%	−5.5%	−6.2%
Goods	SER		0.280	0.273	0.273	−2.5%	0.0%	−2.5%
Domestic	AGF	AGF	0.775	0.815	0.802	5.2%	−1.6%	3.5%
Intermediate	AGF	TEX	0.072	0.272	0.247	277.8%	−9.2%	243.1%
Purchases of	AGF	CHE	0.001	0.002	0.003	100.0%	50.0%	200.0%
Sector *i* from	AGF	MAN	0.011	0.011	0.010	0.0%	−9.1%	−9.1%
Sector *j*	AGF	SER	0.253	0.236	0.240	−6.7%	1.7%	−5.1%

Table 5.1 Policy Scenario Simulation Results (continued).

Variable	*i*	*j*	Value			Per Cent Change		
			Case 0 (Initial)	Case 1	Case 2	Case 0 ⇒ 1	Case 1 ⇒ 2	Case 0 ⇒ 2
	TEX	AGF	0.006	0.007	0.007	16.7%	0.0%	16.7%
	TEX	TEX	0.040	0.149	0.135	272.5%	−9.4%	237.5%
	TEX	CHE	0.001	0.001	0.002	0.0%	100.0%	100.0%
	TEX	MAN	0.008	0.008	0.007	0.0%	−12.5%	−12.5%
	TEX	SER	0.031	0.029	0.029	−6.5%	0.0%	−6.5%
	CHE	AGF	0.062	0.065	0.064	4.8%	−1.5%	3.2%
	CHE	TEX	0.004	0.016	0.014	300.0%	−12.5%	250.0%
	CHE	CHE	0.047	0.056	0.080	19.1%	42.9%	70.2%
	CHE	MAN	0.040	0.040	0.036	0.0%	−10.0%	−10.0%
	CHE	SER	0.137	0.128	0.130	−6.6%	1.6%	−5.1%
	MAN	AGF	0.067	0.070	0.069	4.5%	−1.4%	3.0%
	MAN	TEX	0.004	0.014	0.013	250.0%	−7.1%	225.0%
	MAN	CHE	0.047	0.055	0.080	17.0%	45.5%	70.2%
	MAN	MAN	0.465	0.468	0.419	0.6%	−10.5%	−9.9%
	MAN	SER	0.649	0.606	0.616	−6.6%	1.7%	−5.1%
	SER	AGF	0.443	0.466	0.459	5.2%	−1.5%	3.6%
	SER	TEX	0.044	0.165	0.150	275.0%	−9.1%	240.9%
	SER	CHE	0.095	0.111	0.160	16.8%	44.1%	68.4%
	SER	MAN	0.650	0.655	0.587	0.8%	−10.4%	−9.7%
	SER	SER	2.942	2.749	2.796	−6.6%	1.7%	−5.0%
Foreign Intermediate Purchases of Sector *i* from Sector *j*	AGF	AGF	0.027	0.028	0.028	3.7%	0.0%	3.7%
	AGF	TEX	0.002	0.009	0.008	350.0%	−11.1%	300.0%
	AGF	CHE	0.000	0.000	0.000	N/A	N/A	N/A
	AGF	MAN	0.000	0.000	0.000	N/A	N/A	N/A
	AGF	SER	0.019	0.018	0.018	−5.3%	0.0%	−5.3%
	TEX	AGF	0.003	0.003	0.003	0.0%	0.0%	0.0%
	TEX	TEX	0.036	0.136	0.124	277.8%	−8.8%	244.4%
	TEX	CHE	0.000	0.001	0.001	N/A	0.0%	N/A
	TEX	MAN	0.010	0.010	0.009	0.0%	−10.0%	−10.0%
	TEX	SER	0.008	0.008	0.008	0.0%	0.0%	0.0%
	CHE	AGF	0.036	0.038	0.037	5.6%	−2.6%	2.8%
	CHE	TEX	0.004	0.016	0.015	300.0%	−6.3%	275.0%
	CHE	CHE	0.078	0.092	0.132	17.9%	43.5%	69.2%
	CHE	MAN	0.046	0.046	0.041	0.0%	−10.9%	−10.9%
	CHE	SER	0.088	0.082	0.083	−6.8%	1.2%	−5.7%
	MAN	AGF	0.011	0.012	0.012	9.1%	0.0%	9.1%

Table 5.1 Policy Scenario Simulation Results (continued).

Variable	*i*	*j*	Value			Per Cent Change		
			Case 0 (Initial)	Case 1	Case 2	Case 0⇒1	Case 1⇒2	Case 0⇒2
	MAN	TEX	0.000	0.003	0.003	N/A	0.0%	N/A
	MAN	CHE	0.007	0.008	0.012	14.3%	50.0%	71.4%
	MAN	MAN	0.266	0.268	0.240	0.8%	−10.4%	−9.8%
	MAN	SER	0.137	0.128	0.130	−6.6%	1.6%	−5.1%
	SER	AGF	0.020	0.021	0.021	5.0%	0.0%	5.0%
	SER	TEX	0.002	0.009	0.008	350.0%	−11.1%	300.0%
	SER	CHE	0.002	0.003	0.004	50.0%	33.3%	100.0%
	SER	MAN	0.031	0.031	0.028	0.0%	−9.7%	−9.7%
	SER	SER	0.224	0.210	0.213	−6.3%	1.4%	−4.9%
Price of Intermediate Imports	AGF		1.000	0.967	0.971	−3.3%	0.4%	−2.9%
	TEX		1.000	0.837	0.841	−16.3%	0.5%	−15.9%
	CHE		1.000	0.925	0.929	−7.5%	0.4%	−7.1%
	MAN		1.000	0.923	0.927	−7.7%	0.4%	−7.3%
	SER		1.000	0.989	0.994	−1.1%	0.5%	−0.6%
Supply for Domestic Sales	AGF		1.434	1.655	1.621	15.4%	−2.1%	13.0%
	TEX		0.157	0.256	0.242	63.1%	−5.5%	54.1%
	CHE		0.376	0.387	0.403	2.9%	4.1%	7.2%
	MAN		2.119	2.096	2.074	−1.1%	−1.0%	−2.1%
	SER		7.832	7.794	7.811	−0.5%	0.2%	−0.3%
Supply for Export Sales	AGF		0.802	0.697	0.695	−13.1%	−0.3%	−13.3%
	TEX		0.119	0.780	0.699	555.5%	−10.4%	487.4%
	CHE		0.042	0.104	0.303	147.6%	191.3%	621.4%
	MAN		0.329	0.371	0.134	12.8%	−63.9%	−59.3%
	SER		0.537	0.027	0.141	−95.0%	422.2%	−73.7%
World Price of Exports	AGF		1.000	1.014	1.014	1.4%	0.0%	1.4%
	TEX		1.000	0.991	0.991	−0.9%	0.0%	−0.9%
	CHE		1.000	0.995	0.990	−0.5%	−0.5%	−1.0%
	MAN		1.000	0.999	1.004	−0.1%	0.5%	0.4%
	SER		1.000	1.015	1.007	1.5%	−0.8%	0.7%
Carbon Dioxide Emissions	AGF		4.011	4.207	4.146	4.9%	−1.4%	3.4%
	TEX		0.359	1.145	1.048	218.9%	−8.5%	191.9%
	CHE		2.832	2.971	3.050	4.9%	2.7%	7.7%
	MAN		7.821	7.885	7.121	0.8%	−9.7%	−9.0%
	SER		9.211	8.755	8.871	−5.0%	1.3%	−3.7%

Table 5.1 Policy Scenario Simulation Results (continued).

Variable	i	j	Value			Per Cent Change		
			Case 0 (Initial)	Case 1	Case 2	Case 0 ⇒ 1	Case 1 ⇒ 2	Case 0 ⇒ 2
Production Emissions	AGF		3.785	3.982	3.920	5.2%	−1.6%	3.6%
	TEX		0.283	1.064	0.967	276.0%	−9.1%	241.7%
	CHE		0.383	0.450	0.647	17.5%	43.8%	68.9%
	MAN		7.199	7.255	6.493	0.8%	−10.5%	−9.8%
	SER		6.906	6.454	6.562	−6.5%	1.7%	−5.0%
Total			18.556	19.205	18.589	3.5%	−3.2%	0.2%
Consumption Emissions	AGF		0.226	0.226	0.226	0.0%	0.0%	0.0%
	TEX		0.077	0.082	0.082	6.5%	0.0%	6.5%
	CHE		2.450	2.521	2.403	2.9%	−4.7%	−1.9%
	MAN		0.622	0.630	0.628	1.3%	−0.3%	1.0%
	SER		2.305	2.302	2.308	−0.1%	0.3%	0.1%
Total			5.680	5.761	5.647	1.4%	−2.0%	−0.6%
Total Emissions			24.235	24.964	24.235	3.0%	−2.9%	0.0%
Disposable Income			5.566	5.554	5.587	−0.2%	0.6%	0.4%
Total Production			13.747	14.168	14.125	3.1%	−0.3%	2.7%
Government Revenue			0.080	0.000	0.148	−100.0%	N/A	85.0%
Tariff Revenue			0.080	0.000	0.000	−100.0%	N/A	−100.0%
Carbon Tax Revenue			0.000	0.000	0.148	N/A	N/A	N/A
Exchange Rate			1.000	0.989	0.994	−1.1%	0.5%	−0.6%
Carbon Tax Rate			0.000	0.000	0.006	N/A	N/A	N/A

This results in composite consumption of textiles, chemicals and manufacturing all rising. The fall in import prices is also reflected in the changes in domestic and imported shares of composite consumption. Consumption of domestic goods falls for all five sectors, whereas the consumption of imported goods rises in each sector by between 2.6 per cent and 29.3 per cent. With respect to production, the biggest winner from trade liberalisation is the textiles sector whose output expands by 276.7 per cent, this is accompanied by expansions in the output of agriculture, chemicals and manufacturing of 5.2 per cent, 17.5 per cent and 0.8 per cent, respectively.[2] Services is the only sector to contract with output falling by 6.5 per cent. The total production in the economy rises by 3.1 per cent. Of the increased textiles output, only a small proportion is absorbed domestically, domestic textiles supply rises by 63.1 per cent, with the balance being exported, textiles exports rising by 555.5 per cent. A similar set of results but to a smaller degree can also be seen in the chemicals sector. The opposite result to this is generally true in the agriculture and services sectors. Because of the current account constraint employed in the model, the large increase in textiles and chemicals exports must be offset by a large increase in imports, and/or a significant reduction of exports from other sectors, this effect can be seen in the significant decline in services exports of 95.0 per

[2]It may not be obvious that the biggest winner from trade liberalisation should be the previously protected sector, however this is not unusual given the assumptions employed in the model. Following trade liberalisation, the price of imported textile goods falls, this has an effect on consumption in that more of the composite textile consumption good is foreign-sourced. However, because domestic and foreign goods are treated as imperfect substitutes, this effect is smaller than if had they been treated as perfect substitutes. The fall in the price of imported textile goods also causes the domestic price of textiles production to fall since the cost of foreign-sourced intermediate goods has fallen. This fall in the domestic price of textiles production means that the domestic price is now below the world price of exports, and as such production expands to equilibrate the two prices, with any of the increased production not absorbed domestically being exported. Another assumption which adds to this result is that there is no substitution allowed between domestic and foreign intermediate goods, and as such domestic intermediate demand is higher than when firms substitute cheaper foreign intermediates for domestic intermediates. However, had substitution been allowed, the domestic price would have fallen further, thereby augmenting the increase in production required to equilibrate domestic and world export prices as described above.

cent.[3] It can also be seen that trade liberalisation has led to a 2.7 per cent increase in wages, whereas rents have fallen by 1.1 per cent. These changes on firms result in cost-minimising behaviour which can be seen in the manufacturing sector where the capital stock rises by 1.4 per cent but labour falls by 0.3 per cent despite an increase in production of 0.8 per cent. These changes in wages and rents in combination with the changes in output levels in the textiles and chemicals sectors leads to 275.0 per cent and 274.1 per cent increases in capital and labour in the textiles sector respectively, and 17.5 per cent and 19.4 per cent decreases in capital and labour in the chemicals sector. The value-added or net price increases in all but the manufacturing sector, 1.1 per cent in agricultural products, 1.7 per cent in textiles, 0.6 per cent in chemicals, and 1.3 per cent in the services sector. Because intermediates are simply a linear function of output, these flows all increase or decrease by the same percentage as the output of the sector generating their demand. Trade liberalisation also results in a slight decline in income of 0.2 per cent, and the elimination of tariffs means that government revenue falls by 100 per cent.

Effects on emissions

The generation of emissions in the model also follows a linear form, and as such the production and consumption emissions within any sector are in direct proportion to the output and consumption in that same sector. However production emissions are generated at different rates depending on the sector and so, the expansion of a more polluting sector accompanied by a decline in a less polluting sector, will lead to an increase in overall economy-wide emissions even if total production within the economy has remained constant. This is in fact what has happened to emissions following trade liberalisation. The substantial expansion in output in the textiles sector has resulted in an equally large increase in the production emissions in this sector. The increased production in the agriculture, chemical and manufacturing sectors

[3]This effect occurs more so in the services sector because of the treatment of agricultural exports. Agricultural exports are assumed to have a degree of monopsony power, and as such agricultural exports are not particularly elastic.

also leads to greater production emissions in these sectors. These increases are offset to a small degree by falling production emissions in the services sector. However, because the services sector has the lowest sectoral emissions rate then its contraction means that the increase in total production emissions is in excess of the increase in overall output. As can be seen in Table 5.1, production emissions rise by 5.2 per cent in the agriculture sector, 276.0 per cent in the textiles sector, 17.5 per cent in the chemicals sector and 0.8 per cent in the manufacturing sector, while those in the services sector decline by 6.5 per cent. The total emissions from production in the economy increase by 3.5 per cent, which is slightly greater than the expansion in overall output of 3.1 per cent. Emissions attributable to consumption also rise in the textiles sector by 6.5 per cent due to the increase in consumption, whereas in the services sector they fall by 0.1 per cent. Consumption emissions in the chemicals and manufacturing sectors rise by 2.9 and 1.3 per cent respectively, with those in the agriculture sector remaining unchanged. Overall, total agricultural emissions rise by 4.9 per cent, textiles emissions rise by 218.9 per cent, chemicals emissions rise by 4.9 per cent, manufacturing emissions rise by 0.8 per cent, and services emissions fall by 5.0 per cent, with total economy-wide emissions rising by 3.0 per cent.

Effects on welfare

The effects of trade liberalisation on welfare are well-known, and the expected welfare improvement is also found in this case. Because a Stone-Geary utility function is used as the measure of welfare in this model, the percentage change in its value is not relevant as the utility function is merely ordinal not cardinal.[4] However its value can be used to see if the

---

[4]It is easy enough to construct a measure of the change in welfare, such as equivalent variation or compensating variation, from the Stone-Geary utility function in order to measure how much better or worse off the representative consumer is in the simulated equilibrium (see De Melo & Tarr (1992) for an example of such a measure). However, the purpose of this study is not to investigate how much better or worse off the representative consumer is, but rather whether or not they are better or worse off, as such this specification is sufficient.

representative consumer is better or worse off under the new policy scenario. Following trade liberalisation, it can be seen in Table 5.1 that the representative consumer is in fact made better off, insofar as the utility function includes all factors influencing the representative consumer's welfare. In this case however, that cannot be said since the utility function does not include the level of ambient emissions either as a non-separable or separable effect on preferences. As such, this estimate of welfare is upwardly biased when accompanied by an increase in the level of emissions. Therefore despite the representative consumer appearing to be better off following trade liberalisation, this cannot be said with certainty, and so the effect of trade liberalisation on welfare is ambiguous. Whether the representative consumer is in fact better or worse off following trade liberalisation depends on whether the associated disutility due to the increase in emissions is smaller or greater than the change in utility as measured by the utility function.

Summary of results

It can be seen from the above results that trade liberalisation does lead to a decline in environmental quality in terms of emissions, and as such has an ambiguous effect on welfare. Therefore it cannot be determined at this stage whether trade liberalisation in the absence of a carbon tax is a welfare-enhancing policy strategy.

Case 2: The effects of trade liberalisation in the presence of a carbon tax

The investigation of the effects of trade liberalisation, in the presence of a carbon tax, on emissions and welfare within the CGE model presented in this study can also be performed relatively easily. Following calibration and benchmarking of the model to the initial equilibrium, trade liberalisation in the presence of a carbon tax can be simulated by implementing the model with all tariffs set to zero and by enforcing the relationship given in Equation 4.2.28, where emissions are capped at their 1990 level (as required by the FCCC). This latter constraint is equilibrated by the endogenous carbon tax when generating the new equilibrium. The projected effects of this policy simulation are listed in Table 5.1 above.

The overall effects on the economy of trade liberalisation in the presence of a carbon tax are presented first, this is then followed by a description of the effects on emissions and welfare. Unless otherwise stated, the results presented below refer to the change in endogenous variables between the initial benchmarked equilibrium and the policy simulation in Case 2.

Overall effects on the economy

Just as in Case 1, trade liberalisation leads to a fall in the price of imported intermediate and consumption goods as seen in Table 5.1. In each sector the fall in import prices is slightly smaller that that recorded in Case 1. With the introduction of the carbon tax on both domestic production and consumption prices coupled with the fall in import prices, the price of composite agricultural consumption goods rises by 0.6 per cent, composite chemicals by 4.0 per cent and the price of composite services by 0.4 per cent. Falls in composite consumption prices of 8.3 and 0.9 per cent occur in the textiles and manufacturing sectors, respectively. This results in the composite consumption of textiles rising by 6.3 per cent, composite manufactures by 1.0 per cent, whereas the composite consumption of chemicals falls by 1.7 per cent. These results clearly demonstrate the effect of the imposition of the carbon tax on the chemicals sector. The chemicals sector exhibits a much greater consumption emissions rate that the other four sectors and as such its consumption price is affected to a larger degree. As can be seen in Table 5.1, all sectors composite consumption prices rise from Case 1 to Case 2 by a small degree (0.1 to 1.3 per cent), however the composite chemicals consumption price rises by 9.1 per cent. The fall in import prices is also reflected in the changes in domestic and imported shares of composite consumption. Consumption of domestic goods falls for all but the services sector, whereas the consumption of imported goods rises for all sectors. In terms of production, the biggest winner from trade liberalisation in the presence of a carbon tax is again the textiles sector, however in this case, output expands by a smaller 242.5 per cent. Production in the chemicals sector also expands by 68.9 per cent, which is more than the 17.5 per cent recorded in Case 1. Manufacturing is the most pollution-intensive product and as such is the hardest hit by the imposition of a carbon tax, this effect can be seen in the 9.8 per cent fall in manufacturing output. The total production in the economy rises by 2.7 per cent, this is 0.3 per cent smaller than that recorded in Case 1. Again, as in Case 1 , this increase in textiles output is exported, exports up 487.4 per cent, with domestic supply of textiles also rising by 54.1 per cent. A similar result now also prevails in the chemicals sector with domestic supply increasing by 7.2 per cent and exports increasing by 621.4 per cent. In the agricultural products sector, domestic supply rises by 13.0 per cent, and in this case exports fall by 13.3 per cent. However, in the case of agricultural exports New Zealand has a degree of market power, and as such the fall in exports is offset to a small degree by a rise in the world price of agricultural exports. This fall in agricultural exports, as well as those in the manufacturing and services sectors, can also be attributed to some extent to the current account constraint employed in the model as described in Case 1. It can also be seen that trade liberalisation in the presence of a carbon tax leads to a 1.7 per cent rise in wages, and a 4.4 percent fall in rents, with rents being the hardest hit by the carbon tax. These changes in wages and rents in combination with the changes in output levels lead to a set of results quite similar to those in Case 1 with respect to sectoral capital and labour stocks. The value-added or net price is reduced in all but the textiles sector, with the carbon tax reducing these value-added prices by between 1.2 and 2.7 per cent when compared to Case 1. Because intermediates are simply a linear function of output, then these flows all increase or decrease by the same percentage as the output of the sector generating their demand. The removal of tariffs and the subsequent imposition of a carbon tax results in an increase in government revenue of 85.0 per cent, and an increase in income of 0.4 per cent.

Effects on emissions

In this policy simulation, total emissions are subject to a constraint limiting them to the same level as in the initial benchmarked equilibrium. As such, trade liberalisation in the presence of a carbon tax has no effect on total emissions. However, as mentioned in Case 1 above, production and consumption emissions are generated at different rates in each sector, and because of this, the most pollutive sectors do not expand to the same degree as in Case 1. As can be seen in Table 5.1, production emissions in the agriculture sector rise by 3.6 per cent, 241.7 per cent in the textiles sector, and 68.9 per cent in the chemicals sector, while those in the manufacturing and services sectors decline by 9.8 and 5.0 per cent, respectively. A comparison of the production emissions in this case with those of Case 1 shows that with the imposition of the carbon tax, the least pollutive sectors (namely chemicals and services) have expanded at the expense of the most pollutive sectors. Emissions attributable to consumption rise in the textiles sector by 6.5 per cent, in the manufacturing sector by 1.0 per cent and in the services sector by 0.1 per cent. In the chemicals sector they fall by 1.9 per cent with no change in the agriculture sector. This result when compared with Case 1 again demonstrates how the most consumption pollutive sector, chemicals, is affected the most by the imposition of the carbon tax. Overall, agricultural emissions rise by 3.4 per cent, textiles emissions rise by 191.9 per cent, chemicals emissions rise by 7.7 per cent, manufacturing emissions fall by 9.0 per cent, and services emissions fall by 3.7 per cent, with total economy-wide emissions remaining constant.

Effects on welfare

In the discussion on welfare effects in Case 1 above, it was acknowledged that the use of the utility function in this model lead to a biased estimate of welfare when the level of emissions changed. However, in the policy scenario examined here, the total emissions level remains unchanged through the use of an endogenous emissions tax. Because of this, the utility function can be employed as an unbiased estimate of the level of welfare attained by the representative consumer. The fact that the total level of emissions is unchanged means that there can be no disutility from an increase in emissions and so their effects on welfare can be ignored when we are simply comparing the Case 2 policy simulation with the initial equilibrium. From Table 5.1, it can be seen that trade liberalisation in the presence of a carbon tax is in fact welfare-enhancing, with the level of utility attained being equivalent to that attained in the Case 1 scenario. From this it can be said that the representative consumer is unambiguously made better off through a policy of trade liberalisation in the presence of a carbon tax. Furthermore, because the level of utility attained in this case is equivalent to the level of utility attained in Case 1, it can also be said that the representative consumer is better off under the policy scenario in Case 2 than they are under that of Case 1. This is because although they both produce the same level of utility, Case 1 is also accompanied by an increase in total emissions thereby reducing the effective level of welfare attained.

Summary of results

It can be seen from the above results that trade liberalisation in the presence of a carbon tax has no affect on environmental quality in terms of emissions, and as such unambiguously enhances welfare.[5] Therefore it can be determined that trade liberalisation in the presence of a carbon tax is a superior policy strategy to trade liberalisation in the absence of a carbon tax. In addition to this, it is also apparent that trade liberalisation in the presence of a carbon tax is a superior policy strategy to the protectionist trade policy present in the initial benchmarked case.

[5]This result is supported in theoretical analysis, see Anderson (1992a).

— Chapter 6 —
Summary and Conclusions

Introduction

The objective of this study is to attempt to assess the magnitude of the effects of trade liberalisation on welfare and emissions levels in the New Zealand economy, and the degree to which these effects are influenced by environmental policy. In order to estimate the consequences of trade and environmental policies, a CGE model of the New Zealand economy incorporating a trade and environment focus is constructed. Such a model was developed which incorporated the key trade and environmental characteristics and features of the New Zealand economy, which made it suitable for the analysis of trade and environmental policy scenarios. This model was then used to analyse the impacts of the two policy scenarios, trade liberalisation in the absence of a carbon tax, and trade liberalisation in the presence of a carbon tax. While acknowledging that the estimation of these effects using the CGE model employed in this study should be used to complement other approaches to their estimation, the application of the model does show this method to be valuable for developing policy responses. In this sense the relevance of this study is not solely confined to the case of New Zealand, but has implications for many other small open market-based economies contemplating freer trade policies.

Major Findings

The survey of the literature on trade and the environment conducted in this study has served several purposes. It has identified the reasons why trade can affect the environment, and has presented a summary of the interactions between trade and environmental policies. The political economy of protection has been reviewed and the related evidence presented. A description of how international trade can affect the environment has also been given, with evidence relating to environmental policy and competitiveness, as well as the pollution haven hypothesis, being shown. In addition, the effects of trade liberalisation on the environment have also been detailed, and the respective evidence reviewed. The result of this survey is that the evidence relating to trade and environment issues is predominantly theoretical in nature and as such the need for further empirical and computational work has been identified.

The main focus of this study was to assess the effects of trade liberalisation both in the presence, and in the absence of a carbon tax, on the environment (emissions) and welfare. The results of these two policy scenarios, namely, the effects of trade liberalisation in the absence of a carbon tax, and, the effects of trade liberalisation in the presence of a carbon tax have resulted in the following effects being identified with respect to emissions and welfare. Trade liberalisation on its own is found to have an adverse effect on the level of emissions, with total emissions increasing by 3.0 per cent. When the impact of this increase in emissions on welfare is ignored, welfare is seen to rise following trade liberalisation, however when the impact of increased emissions is considered, the effect on welfare is ambiguous. The simulation of trade liberalisation in the presence of an endogenous carbon tax maintaining the emissions level, is on the other hand, found to have an unambiguous positive effect on welfare, with emissions remaining constant.

These results demonstrate that trade liberalisation when accompanied by environmental policy leads to superior welfare and environmental outcomes than does trade liberalisation in the absence of an accompanying environmental policy. In addition, environmental policy seems to have no affect on the size of the gains from trade liberalisation. Furthermore, the policy of trade liberalisation accompanied by environmental policy is also seen to generate superior welfare outcomes than the present protectionist trade policy, while leaving the environment unaffected.

The results obtained in this study compare favourably with those found by Smith & Espinosa (1995), as well as those reported by Beghin,

Roland-Holst & van der Mensbrugghe (1995). Both of these studies find trade liberalisation, when considered alone, to have a negative effect on the environment, and trade liberalisation when accompanied by environmental policy to be environmentally beneficial and welfare-enhancing. The results presented in this study are also consistent with those based on theoretical analyses, such as that of Anderson (1992a), who showed that "... there is an unambiguous welfare gain from trade for a small country provided something approaching the optimal environmental policy is also introduced ...". Furthermore, the hypotheses that trade policies are a poor substitute for environmental policies, and that trade liberalisation is welfare-enhancing in the presence of these environmental policies, have been confirmed in this analysis.

Policy implications

The results of the two policy simulations as presented above have clear-cut policy implications, both for New Zealand, and more generally for other small market-based economies contemplating liberalised trade regimes.

It is apparent from the results that the use of trade policy (namely tariffs) to protect the environment is second best. Furthermore, the results clearly demonstrate that the optimal policy is one of trade liberalisation accompanied by an environmental policy. It has been shown that this policy can realise all the gains from trade liberalisation without compromising environmental quality. Trade liberalisation on its own does lead to environmental degradation. However, these negative environmental effects are shown to exist only when there is a lack of appropriate environmental policies in place. As such it can reasonably be concluded that there is nothing to fear from trade liberalisation with respect to the environment, provided an appropriate environmental policy is present. Therefore New Zealand's policy of continued trade liberalisation is unlikely to have serious environmental impacts (in terms of carbon dioxide emissions), given that the implementation of a carbon tax is expected in the near term.[1]

[1]See Working Group on CO_2 Policy (1996).

These results are also applicable to other small market-based economies, proposing more liberal trade policies. The results presented above indicate that a policy of trade liberalisation should not produce serious negative environmental effects provided appropriate environmental policies are in place. However, should the environmental effects of trade liberalisation be ignored, resulting in inadequate environmental policies, then trade liberalisation is likely to have negative environmental effects, and as such, welfare may deteriorate. Furthermore, if these effects are ignored, then liberalising countries run the risk of losing support for trade liberalisation as it becomes increasingly associated with environmental degradation. As such, these small economies should consider the implementation of co-ordinated trade and environmental policies. It is clear from the results presented above that this co-ordination of trade and environmental policies is a "win-win" situation as there is nothing to lose (in terms of the gains from trade liberalisation and welfare) from the implementation of appropriate environmental policies when liberalising trade.

Limitations and Possible Extensions

Despite the fact that CGE modelling is becoming more and more popular, it should be noted that these types of models are not without their limitations. These limitations exist in two main areas, the specification of the model's theoretical structure, and the database used for the empirical estimation of the model.

The theoretical structure of the model is based on De Melo & Tarr's model of the US economy and incorporates well-accepted neo-classical assumptions. However, the model used for the analysis in this study does possess some limitations worth highlighting. The model includes a higher level of aggregation than desired, which reduces the scope for sector-specific analysis of the results of the policy scenario simulations. In terms of the empirical estimation the model utilised elasticity parameters and coefficients reported in other CGE models, rather than estimates developed specifically for the model. Econometric estimation of these parameters would be the ideal solution, however, this was beyond the scope of this study.

There are also several areas where the model could be extended to provide improved simulation results. The treatment of intermediate goods could be expanded to incorporate energy and non-energy intermediate inputs, where energy inputs are a nested CES composite of various energy types. This would also enable emissions rates to be attributed to the use of each type of energy input, and would in turn, mean that firms could substitute away from energy inputs with high emissions rates upon the imposition of an emissions tax. Furthermore substitution possibilities could also be allowed between value-added and the composite energy input.[2] The modelling of emissions from consumption is incorporated in the present study, however the data used was limited by a high degree of sectoral aggregation. Improvements could be made by utilising consumption emissions data at a more disaggregated level. The modelling of emissions could also be extended to include other ambient emissions such as sulphur oxides, nitrogen oxides and particulate matter, as well as non-ambient emissions such as effluents.[3] Another area where emissions modelling could be enhanced is the modelling of carbon dioxide sequestration by forestry, this would enable the effects of policies on net emissions to be modelled. A common limitation of static CGE models, such as the model employed in this study, is that technology is treated as exogenous. The introduction of dynamic behaviour into the model would allow improvements in technology, which is a particularly important factor in the determination of emission rates.

An additional extension of this model could be its application to other countries. Because of the neoclassical specification of the model it would require few if any changes to the equations, as well as a suitable consistent database including parameter specifications, in order for it to be applied to another economy, or group of countries progressing towards a more liberalised trade regime.

---

[2]This approach was followed by Beghin, Roland-Holst & van der Mensbrugghe (1995).

[3]Smith and Espinosa (1995) incorporate emissions of sulphur oxides, nitrogen oxides and particulate matter.

Conclusion

This study has developed a CGE model of the New Zealand economy, incorporating a trade and environment focus, in order to examine the effects of trade liberalisation on the environment and welfare both with and without an accompanying environmental policy. The results have demonstrated that trade liberalisation when accompanied by environmental policy leads to superior welfare and environmental outcomes than does trade liberalisation in the absence of an accompanying environmental policy. The imposition of an environmental policy is also seen to have no significant impact on the size of the gains from trade liberalisation. Furthermore, it is demonstrated that trade liberalisation when accompanied by an environmental policy also results in superior welfare outcomes than the present protectionist trade policy, while leaving the environment unaffected. The relevance of this study's results are not confined only to the case of New Zealand, but have implications for many other small open market-based economies who have demonstrated a commitment to trade liberalisation.

— *Appendix A* —
Data Set Construction, Model Calibration and Elasticity Specification

This appendix describes the data set construction and calibration calculations used to obtain the benchmark equilibrium for counterfactual simulations, and the sources and specification of elasticities. A schematic representation of the steps involved can be seen in Figure A.1. Minimal data manipulation was required due to the availability of data that closely conformed to the needs for this study. These data sources and manipulations are described below, and are followed by a discussion of the process involved in calibrating the model and the elasticities employed in the model.

Data Set and Data Sources

In order for the model to be implemented, economy-wide data was needed at the five-sector level. The construction of this data set started with Philpott and Nana's 1990 inter-industry table with disaggregated agriculture, which was used as the database for the Julianne model.[1] This database was produced at a 26-sector level and the mapping of these sectors into the five used in the model can be seen in Table A.1.

[1]See Philpott and Nana (1993). For details of the Julianne model, see Stroombergen and Philpott (1980, 1981).

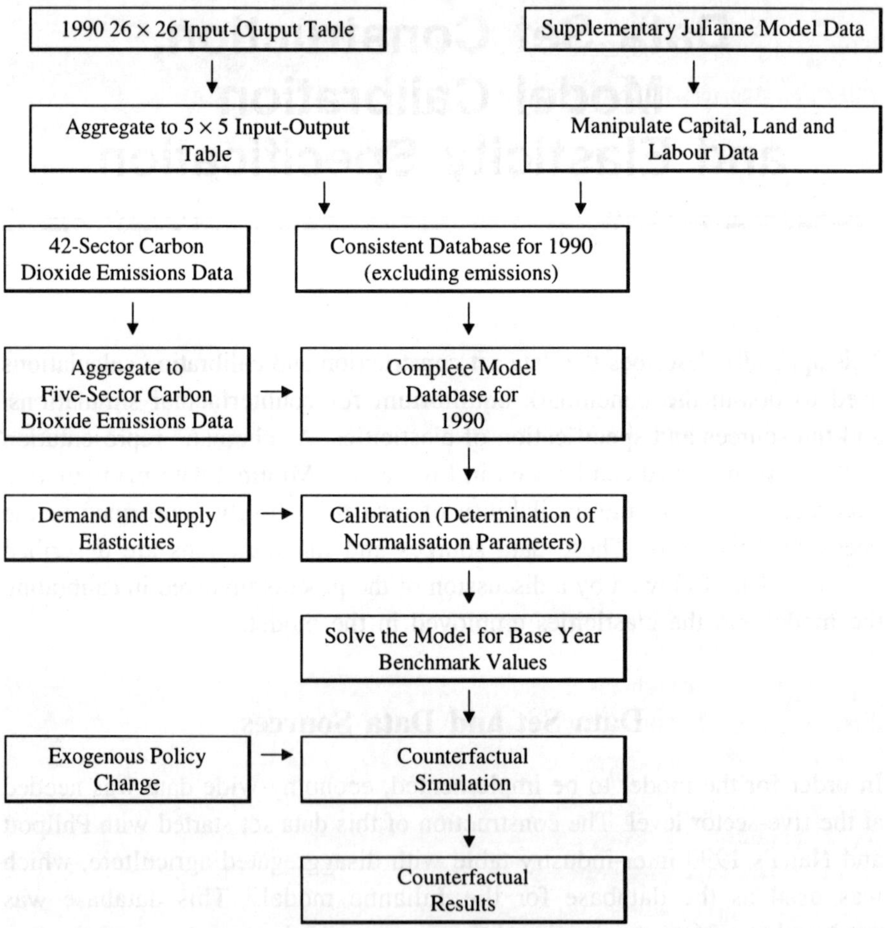

Figure A.1 Benchmarking.

Table A.1 Mapping of 26-Sector Data into Five Sectors.

Sectors in 26-Industry Database	Sectors in Five-Industry Model
1 Dairy Farming; Sheep and Beef Farming; Other Agriculture; Fishing; Meat Processing; Dairy Processing; Other Food, Beverages and Tobacco.	Agriculture and Food (AGF)
2 Textiles, Apparel and Leather	Textiles (TEX)
3 Chemicals	Chemicals (CHE)
4 Forestry and Logging; Mining and Quarrying; Wood and Wood Products; Paper, Printing and Publishing; Ceramics; Basic Metals; Fabricated Metal Products and Manufacturing; Other Manufacturing, Ownership of Dwellings.	Manufacturing (MAN)
5 Electricity, Gas and Water; Building and Construction; Trade, Restaurants and Hotels; Transport and Storage; Communications; Finance, Insurance and Real Estate; Private Services; Public Services.	Services and Other Industries (SER)

In the Philpott & Nana database, land stocks and land rentals are also given. Since this study does not incorporate land in the production function, then these could have either been discarded or treated as another form of capital. The approach taken here is the latter and as such capital stocks in this study are the sum of capital and land stocks in the source database.[2]

Because the data from Philpott & Nana contained sectoral factor rewards, and the model in this study utilises factor rewards that are equal over the whole economy then the capital and labour stocks needed to be adjusted to account for this difference. The process followed to achieve this was relatively simple, whereby the sectoral capital and labour stocks employed in this study are simply the product of the factor stocks and factor rewards

[2]It should be noted that land was treated as a factor of production in only three of the 26 sectors in the Philpott & Nana database, namely Dairy Farming, Sheep and Cattle, and Other Agriculture.

in the Philpott & Nana database. This results in factor rewards in this study being initially calibrated to unity.

The treatment of tariffs and duties differs slightly in this study to that of the Julianne model, and as such the values of imports in the source data

Table A.2 Data Set Matrix.

N_{ij}^d	AGF	TEX	CHE	MAN	SER	Total, N_i^d	C_i^d	E_i	X_i
AGF	7744.2	723.0	14.8	110.9	2529.9	11122.8	3212.7	8022.6	22358.1
TEX	63.9	395.4	11.5	80.7	308.3	859.8	706.6	1187	2753.4
CHE	617.9	41.8	473.8	401.6	1367.7	2902.8	852.9	419.6	4175.3
MAN	670.0	38.1	470.8	4645.7	6487.1	12311.7	8882.9	3292.7	24487.3
SER	4430.8	438.8	945.2	6502.9	29421.4	41739.1	36578.5	5373.5	83691.1
Total, N_j^d	13526.8	1637.1	1916.1	11741.8	40114.4	68936.2	50233.6	18295.4	137465.2

N_{ij}^m	AGF	TEX	CHE	MAN	SER	Total, N_i^m	C_i^m
AGF	269.2	22.7	0.0	0.1	190.1	482.1	552.6
TEX	27.0	362.5	8.8	98.3	81.3	577.9	576.1
CHE	358.6	42.7	778.1	455.3	875.4	2510.0	896.6
MAN	112.4	7.8	69.7	2664.2	1366.3	4220.4	1502.3
SER	200.3	23.8	22.6	306.2	2242.3	2795.1	1900.5
Total, N_j^m	967.5	459.4	879.1	3524.1	4755.4	10585.5	5428.1

	AGF	TEX	CHE	MAN	SER	Total
K_j	3094.1	117.4	724.8	6289.1	13917.2	24142.6
L_j	4769.8	539.5	655.3	2932.3	24904.1	33800.9

X_j	22358.1	2753.4	4175.3	24487.3	83691.1	137465.2

Note: (Columns may not sum correctly due to rounding errors.)

does not include the duty paid. This meant that the import data needed to be scaled to add the tariff duties on imported intermediates and consumption goods. This modification is merely cosmetic and affects the consistency of the data set in no way.

Since this model does not attempt to model investment behaviour, then the investment data from Philpott & Nana was removed from the data set employed here.

Carbon dioxide emissions data

Carbon dioxide emissions data was obtained from the Ministry of Commerce and gives emissions through fuel use for 42 sectors. These sectors were then mapped into the five classes included in this study, and production emissions rates ϕ_i^x calculated. This was done by dividing the sectoral emissions due to production by production in those sectors, as seen in Equation A.1.

$$\phi_i^x = \frac{Z_i^x}{X_i} \tag{A.1}$$

In the case of consumption emissions, the emissions were divided into only two sectors — chemicals and non-chemicals emissions. As such, all sectors have an identical emissions rate except for the chemicals sector. This means that consumption emissions and a carbon tax on these emissions will have an effect on consumption prices at the margin.

$$\phi_i^c = \frac{Z^c}{\sum_{i=1}^{n} C_i} \tag{A.2}$$

Tariffs

The tariff rates used in this model were taken from Philpott & Nana (1993), where they were calculated as the weighted average with respect to imports when aggregating the 26 sectors into the five used here.

Table A.3 Carbon Dioxide Emissions Data.

Sector	Production Emissions Z^x	ϕ_i^x	Sector	Consumption Emissions Z^c	ϕ_i^c
AGF	3.784787	1.692803503	CHE	2.450000	14.004238883
TEX	0.282575	1.026276603	Non-CHE	3.229683	0.599063655
CHE	0.382682	0.916537734			
MAN	7.199252	2.939994201			
SER	6.906400	0.825225143			
Total	18.555696	1.349846798	Total	5.679683	1.020096282

Table A.4 Tariffs by Sector.

Sector	Tariff Rate % (*ad valorem*)
AGF	2.27
TEX	18.20
CHE	6.90
MAN	7.17
SER	0.00

Model Calibration

The calibration determines the values of the normalisation parameters so as to replicate the observed data set. As discussed above, it is assumed that factors earn equal rewards in different sectors.

The calibration starts with the choice of units, prices inclusive of tariffs are set to unity as are factor rewards and the exchange rate:

$$\begin{aligned} P_i^d &= 1.0\,, \\ P_i^{nm} = P_i^{cm} &= 1.0\,, \\ W = R &= 1.0\,, \\ ER &= 1.0\,, \end{aligned} \tag{A.3}$$

From this choice of units, given tariff rates t_i^{nm} and t_i^{cm}, one can solve for the world price of traded goods P_i^{we}, P_i^{wnm} and P_i^{wcm} from Equations 4.2.11, 4.2.12 and 4.2.13 in Chapter 4.

Constant returns to scale (CRS)

In calibrating the CES functions, the general form is defined below with all CES functions being calibrated analogously:

$$X = \overline{A}\left[\delta X_1^{-\rho} + (1-\delta)X_2^{-\rho}\right]^{\frac{-1}{\rho}} \tag{A.4}$$

where the sector subscripts are dropped. The first-order condition can then be re-written as:

$$\delta = \left[1 + \left(\frac{X_1}{X_2}\right)^{\rho - 1}\frac{P_2}{P_1}\right]^{-1} \quad \text{where} \quad \sigma = \frac{1}{1-\rho} \tag{A.5}$$

where P_1 and P_2 are the prices corresponding to X_1 and X_2, and the value of ρ is given by the elasticity of substitution. Under CRS the prices are unity by choice of units above, and the values of X_1, X_2 and X are those of the initial data. The solution of Equation A.5 for δ ensures that the first-order conditions hold in the initial equilibrium. Given the value of δ, the solution of Equation A.4 for $\overline{A}$, guarantees the CES equations hold in the initial equilibrium. Then, the unit prices for the CES aggregator functions can be determined and similarly the value-added price.

The γ_i^c parameters from the consumer demand function represent the minimum subsistence requirements. By defining *Frisch* as:

$$Frisch = \frac{-Y}{(Y - \sum_{j=1}^{n}\gamma_j^c P_j^c)} \tag{A.6}$$

then

$$\gamma_i^c = C_i + \left(\frac{\beta_i}{P_i^c}\right)\left(\frac{Y}{Frisch}\right) \tag{A.7}$$

As detailed below, the values of the β_i parameters are derived from the elasticities. The value of the *Frisch* parameter used above was equal to −1.82, which is the same value employed in the ORANI model of Australia.[3] Given the β_i values, the *Frisch* value, $P_i^c \equiv 1$ by choice of units, and initial data for C_i, γ_i^c can be calculated from Equation A.7.

Elasticity Sources and Specification

Elasticity of substitution between capital and labour

Caddy (1976) surveys estimates of the elasticity of substitution between capital and labour and finds they generally fall in the range 0.5 and 1.0, with time-series estimates generally around 0.5 and cross-section estimates generally around 1.0. Caddy also finds it difficult to rationalise the assignment of different elasticities to different industries. Since this study has a long-term time horizon, the elasticity of substitution between capital and labour assigned to all sectors is 0.5. This assignment is the same as that used in the ORANI model.[3]

Elasticity of substitution between imported and domestic final products

The assignment of the elasticities of substitution between imported and domestic final (consumption) products were taken from the ORANI model of Australia, where the values were taken from the sectors conforming closest to those used in this study.[3] It should be noted that these elasticities are not ordinary uncompensated own-elasticity of demand, because in the derivation of Equation A.8 the cost of producing a fixed level of output was minimised. So these elasticities are similar to a compensated elasticity of demand because the firm stays on the same isoquant in response to a price change (De Melo & Tarr, 1992).

[3]See Dixon *et al.* (1982).

$$\frac{C_i^m}{C_i^d} = \left(\frac{\delta_i^c}{1-\delta_i^c}\right)^{\sigma_i^c} \left(\frac{P_i^d}{P_i^{cm}}\right)^{\sigma_i^c} \tag{A.8}$$

Elasticity of demand for composite final goods

The consumer demand equation in the model has five β_i and five γ_i^c parameters, with the remaining values being initial equilibrium data. As discussed above, once the β_i values are given the γ_i^c values are determined by the assumption of initial equilibrium. Therefore to obtain the β_i value, all that is required are the five elasticities and the *Frisch* parameter.

In calibrating the β_i parameters, any value of β_i can be chosen so that the implied own-price elasticities are consistent with literature estimates of either price or income elasticities. Here, the latter process as chosen by De Melo & Tarr (1992) is followed, using Equation A.9 below, where ε_i^Y is the income elasticity.

$$\varepsilon_i^Y = \frac{\beta_i Y}{P_i^c C_i} \tag{A.9}$$

The elasticities are based on those reported in De Melo & Tarr (1992), which in turn are based on the work of Lluch, Powell & Williams (1977) who estimated a consumption function of composite consumption with an identical top-level consumption structure to that employed in this study. Lluch *et al.* found a pattern of income elasticities that was consistent with restrictions imposed by utility theory. The income elasticities for this study were taken from the closest comparable sector in De Melo & Tarr, and were normalised so that their weighted average satisfied the Engel aggregation condition (otherwise Walras' law will fail to hold in general equilibrium).

Elasticity of demand for exports

The elasticities of demand for exports are based on the assumption that New Zealand has monopsony power only in the agricultural goods sector

Table A.5 Elasticities.

Sector	Elasticity of Substitution between Capital and Labour	Elasticity of Substitution between Imported and Domestic Final Products	Elasticities of Demand for Composite Final Goods	Elasticities of Demand for Exports
AGF	0.5	1.5	0.30	10.0
TEX	0.5	2.5	1.15	200.0
CHE	0.5	2.0	1.06	200.0
MAN	0.5	2.0	1.06	200.0
SER	0.5	2.0	1.05	200.0

Note: CES functions imply that the corresponding elasticities of substitution correspond to compensated demand elasticities (see De Melo & Tarr, 1992).

and as such has a low elasticity only in this sector. The assignment of the elasticities of demand for exports are similar to those in the ORANI model of Australia, where the values were taken from the sectors conforming closest to those used in this study.[3]

Because the elasticities utilised in this study are borrowed from other studies in which sensitivity analysis was performed, this procedure was deemed unnecessary in this case. For example, De Melo & Tarr (1992) specify high, central and low elasticities, and it is these central elasticities that are applied in this study. For details of this sensitivity analysis and justification of the elasticities employed, see Dixon *et al.* (1982) and De Melo & Tarr (1992).

— Bibliography —

Anderson, K. (1992a), The Standard Welfare Economics of Policies Affecting Trade and the Environment, in Anderson, K. and R. Blackhurst (eds.), *The Greening of World Trade Issues* (Harvester, New York).

Anderson, K. (1992b), Agricultural Trade Liberalisation and the Environment: A Global Perspective, *The World Economy* 15(1), 153–171.

Anderson, K. and R. Blackhurst (eds.) (1992), *The Greening of World Trade Issues* (Harvester, New York).

Armington, P. (1969), A Theory of Demand for Products Distinguished by Place of Origin, *IMF Staff Papers* 16, 159–178.

Arrow, K. and G. Debreu (1954), Existence of an Equilibrium for a Competitive Process, *Econometrica* 22, 265–290.

Arrow, K. and F. Hahn (1971), *General Competitive Analysis* (Holden Day, San Francisco).

Asako, K. (1979), Environmental Pollution in an Open Economy, *Economic Record* 55, 359–367.

Baldwin, R. (1993), *Does Sustainability Require Growth?*, Paper presented at the Joint CEPR/OECD Development Centre Conference on Sustainable Economic Development, Paris.

Bandara, J. (1991), Computable General Equilibrium Models for Development Policy Analysis in LDCs, *Journal of Economic Surveys* 5(1), 3–69.

Barbier, E. (1994), Les Effets Environnementaux des Échanges dans le Secteur Forestier, in *Les Effets Environnementaux des Échanges*, OECD.

Barde, J.P. (1994), *Economic Instruments in Environmental Policy: Lessons from the OECD Experience and Their Relevance to Developing Countries*, OECD Development Centre Technical Papers No. 92.

Baumol, W. and W. Oates (1988), *The Theory of Environmental Policy* (Prentice Hall, New Jersey).

Beghin, J., D. Roland-Holst and D. van der Mensbrugghe (1994a), A Survey of the Trade and Environment Nexus: Global Dimensions, *OECD Economic Studies* 23, 167–192.

Beghin, J., D. Roland-Holst and D. van der Mensbrugghe (1994b), *Trade and Pollution Linkages: Piecemeal Reform and Optimal Intervention*, OECD Development Centre Technical Papers No. 99.

Beghin J., D. Roland-Holst and D. van der Mensbrugghe (1995), Trade Liberalisation and the Environment in the Pacific Basin: Co-ordinated Approaches to Mexican Trade and Environment Policy, *American Journal of Agricultural Economics* 77, 778–785.

Bell, C. (1990), Reforming Property Rights in Land and Tenancy, *The World Bank Research Observer* 5(2), 143–166.

Bhagwati, J. (1981), The Generalised Theory of Distortions and Welfare, in Bhagwati, J. (ed.), *International Trade: Selected Readings* (Cambridge, MIT Press).

Binswanger, H.P., K. Deininger and G. Feder (1993), Agricultural Land Relations in the Developing World, *American Journal of Agricultural Economics* 75, 1242–1248.

Birdsall, N. and D. Wheeler (1992), Trade Policy and Industrial Pollution in Latin America: Where are the Pollution Havens?, in Low, P. (ed.), *International Trade and the Environment* (World Bank, Washington D.C.).

Blackhurst, R. (1977), International Trade and Domestic Environmental Policies in a Growing World Economy, in Blackhurst, R. *et al.* (eds.), *International Relations in a Changing World* (Sythoff-Leiden, Geneva).

Blackhurst, R. and A. Subramanian (1992), Promoting Multilateral Co-operation on the Environment, in Anderson, K. and R. Blackhurst (eds.), *The Greening of World Trade Issues* (Harvester, New York).

Blackorby C., D. Primont and R. Russel (1978), *Duality, Separability and Functional Structure: Theory and Economic Applications* (North-Holland, Amsterdam).

Boado, E. (1988), Incentive Policies and Forest Use in the Philippines, in Repetto, R. and M. Gillis (eds.), *Public Policies and the Misuse of Forest Resources* (Cambridge University Press, Cambridge).

Bohm, P. (1992), Distributional Implications of Allowing International Trade in CO_2 Emission Quotas, *The World Economy* 15, 107–114.

Bohm, P. (1993), *Should Marginal Carbon Abatement Costs be Equalised Across Countries?*, Working Paper, Department of Economics, University of Stockholm.

Bohm, P. and C.S. Russell (1985), Comparative Analysis of Alternative Policy Instruments, in Kneese, A.V. and J.L. Sweeney (eds.), *Handbook of Natural Resource and Energy Economics* (North-Holland, Amsterdam).

Borges, A. (1986), Applied General Equilibrium Models: An Assessment of Their Usefulness for Policy Analysis, *OECD Economic Studies* 7, 7–43.

Braga, C.A.P. (1992), Tropical Forests and Trade Policy: The Case of Indonesia and Brazil, in Low, P. (ed.), *International Trade and the Environment*, World Bank Discussion Paper No. 159 (World Bank, Washington D.C).

Brooke, A., D. Kendrick and A. Meeraus (1992), *Gams: A User's Guide, Release 2.25* (Boyd and Fraser, Massachusetts).

Bureau of Industry Economics (1989), *Trade Liberalisation and Australian Manufacturing Industry — The Impact of the Australia–New Zealand CER Trade Agreement*, Research Report 29 (Australian Government Publishing Service, Canberra).

Burniaux, J.-M. *et al.* (1992), GREEN: A Global Model for Quantifying the Costs of Policies to Curb CO_2 Emissions, *OECD Economic Studies* 19, 49–92.

Caddy, V. (1976), *Empirical Estimation of the Elasticity of Substitution: A Review*, Preliminary Working Paper OP-09, Impact Project, Industries Assistance Commission, Melbourne, Australia.

Chivers, M. (1995), *Greenhouse Gas Emissions from New Zealand Energy Sources 1990–1993* (Ministry of Commerce, Wellington).

Chung, J. (1994), *Utility and Production Functions: Theory and Applications* (Blackwell, Cambridge).

Cook, Z. and J. Tobey (1992), *Agricultural Protection and the Environment: A Comparative Analysis*, processed, USDA-ERS and OECD Environment Directorate.

Copeland, B.R. (1991), International Trade in Waste Products in the Presence of Illegal Disposal, *Journal of Environmental Economic and Management* 20, 143–162.

Copeland, B.R. (1993), *Process Standards, Pollution Content Taxes, and the Control of Cross-Border Pollution*, University of British Columbia Discussion Paper 93-42.

Copeland, B.R. (1994), International Trade and the Environment: Policy Reform in a Polluted Small Economy, *Journal of Environmental Economics and Management* 26, 44–65.

Copeland, B.R. and S.M. Taylor (1993), *Trade and Transboundary Pollution*, University of British Columbia Discussion Paper 93-46.

Copeland, B.R. and S.M. Taylor (1994), North-South Trade and the Environment, *Quarterly Journal of Economics* 109, 755–787.

Copeland, B.R. and S.M. Taylor (1995), Trade and the Environment: A Partial Synthesis, *American Journal of Agriculture Economics* 77, 765–771.

D'Arge, R. (1974), International Trade, Domestic Income, and Environmental Controls, in Kneese, A. (ed.), *Managing the Environment* (Praeger, New York).

Deacon, R. (1992), *Controlling Tropical Deforestation: An Analysis of Alternative Policies*, processed, University of California, Santa Barbara.

Dean A. and P. Hoeller (1992), Costs of Reducing CO_2 Emissions: Evidence from Six Global Models, *OECD Economic Studies* 19, 15–48.

Dean, J. (1992), Trade and Environment: A Survey of the Literature, in Low, P. (ed.), *International Trade and the Environment* (World Bank, Washington D.C.).

Dean, J. (1996), *Testing the Impact of Trade Liberalisation on the Environment*, Draft Working Paper (August 1996).

Dervis, K., J. de Melo and S. Robinson (1982), *General Equilibrium Models for Development Policy* (World Bank, Cambridge University Press, Cambridge).

Devarajan, S. (1995), Environment and Trade in General Equilibrium: Theory, Methodology, and Evidence: Discussion, *American Journal of Agricultural Economics* 77, 786–788.

Devarajan, S., J. Lewis and S. Robinson (1990), Policy Lessons from Trade-Focused, Two-Sector Models, *Journal of Policy Modelling* 12, 625–657.

Diwan, I. and N. Shafik (1992), Towards a North-South Deal on the Environment, in Low, P. (ed.), *International Trade and the Environment* (World Bank, Washington D.C.).

Dixon, P., B. Parmenter, J. Sutton and D. Vincent (1982), *ORANI: A Multisectoral Model of the Australian Economy* (North-Holland, Amsterdam).

Drake-Brockman, J. and K. Anderson (1994), *The Trade/Environment Debate and Its Implications for Asia-Pacific*, paper prepared for the Australian Committee of the Pacific Economic Co-operation Council (AUSPECC), Centre for International Economic Studies, University of Adelaide.

Emerson, P. and R. Mickesell (1991), *North American Free Trade: A Survey of Environmental Concerns*, Policy Briefing, Pacific Research Institute, San Francisco.

Espinosa J. and V. Smith (1995), Measuring the Environmental Consequences of Trade Policy: A Non-Market CGE Analysis, *American Journal of Agricultural Economics* 77, 772–777.

Gale, S. (1990), *The New Zealand Experience of Liberalisation and Deregulation*, Working Paper 90/13 (NZIER, Wellington).

Gillis, M. (1988a), Indonesia: Public Policies, Resource Management, and the Tropical Forest, in Repetto, R. and M. Gillis (eds.), *Public Policies and the Misuse of Forest Resources* (Cambridge University Press, Cambridge).

Gillis, M. (1988b), Malaysia: Public Policies and the Tropical Forest, in Repetto, R. and M. Gillis (eds.), *Public Policies and the Misuse of Forest Resources* (Cambridge University Press, Cambridge).

Gillis, M. (1988c), West Africa: Resource Management Policies and the Tropical Forest, in Repetto, R. and M. Gillis (eds.), *Public Policies and the Misuse of Forest Resources* (Cambridge University Press, Cambridge).

Globerman, S. (1993), The Environmental Impacts of Trade Liberalisation, in Anderson, T., *NAFTA and the Environment* (Pacific Research Institute for Public Policy, San Francisco).

Grossman, G.M. (1993), *Pollution and Growth: What Do We Know?*, Paper presented at the Joint Centre for Economic Policy Research/OECD Development Centre Conference on Sustainable Economic Development: Domestic and International Policy, Paris.

Grossman, G.M., and A.B. Krueger (1992), *Environmental Impacts of a North American Free Trade Agreement*, CEPR Discussion Paper 644.

Grubel, H. and P. Lloyd (1975), *Intra-Industry Trade: The Theory and Measurement of International Trade in Differentiated Products* (Macmillan and Halsted, London).

Hahn, R.W. (1990), The Political Economy of Environmental Regulation: Towards A Unifying Framework, *Public Choice* 65, 21–47.

Haines, A. and C. Fuchs (1991), Potential Impacts on Health of Atmospheric Change, *Journal of Public Health Medicine* 13(2), 69–80.

Hettige, H., R. Lucas and D. Wheeler (1992), The Toxic Intensity of Industrial Production: Global Patterns, Trends, and Trade Policy, *American Economic Review, Papers and Proceedings* 82, 478–481.

Hewison G. (1995), *Reconciling Trade and the Environment: Issues for New Zealand* (Institute of Policy Studies, Victoria University of Wellington).

Hillman, A.L., and H.W. Ursprung (1992), The Influence of Environmental Concerns on Political Determination of Trade Policy, in Anderson, K. and R. Blackhurst (eds.), *The Greening of World Trade Issues* (Harvester, New York).

Hoekman, B. and M. Leidy (1992), Environmental Policy Formation in a Trading Economy: A Public Choice Perspective, in Anderson, K. and R. Blackhurst (eds.), *The Greening of World Trade Issues* (Harvester, New York).

International Food Policy Research Institute (IFPRI) (1990), *Environmental Aspects of Agricultural Development*, IFPRI Policy Briefs 6.

International Energy Agency (1994), *Climate Change Update 1994* (IEA).

Isard, P. (1978), How Far Can One Push the Law of One Price?, *American Economic Review* 67, 942–948.

Johnson, H. (1960), The Costs of Protection and the Scientific Tariff, *Journal of Political Economy* 68, 327–345.

Kennaway, R. and J. Henderson (eds.) (1992), *Beyond New Zealand II — Foreign Policy into the 1990s* (Longman Paul, Auckland).

Klepper, G. (1992), The Political Economy of Trade and the Environment in Western Europe, in Low, P. (ed.), *International Trade and the Environment* (World Bank, Washington).

Krutilla, K. (1991), Environmental Regulation in an Open Economy, *Journal of Environmental Economics and Management* 20, 127–142.

Leaf, A. (1989), Potential Health Effects of Global Climatic and Environmental Changes, *The New England Journal of Medicine* 321(23), 1577–1583.

Leamer, E. and R. Stern (1970), *Quantitive International Economics* (Boston, Allyn and Bacon).

Lee, H. and D. Roland-Holst (1994), International Trade and the Transfer of Environmental Costs and Benefits, in Francois, J. and K. Reinert (eds.), *Applied Trade Policy Modelling* (Cambridge University Press, Cambridge).

Leonard, J. (1988), *Pollution and the Struggle for the World Product* (Cambridge University Press, New York).

Lloyd, P. (1992), The Problem of Optimal Environmental Policy Choice, in Anderson, K. and R. Blackhurst (eds.), *The Greening of World Trade Issues* (Harvester, New York).

Lluch, C., A. Powell and R. Williams (1977), *Patterns in Household Demand and Savings* (Oxford University Press, Oxford).

Lopez, R. (1992), The Environment as a Factor of Production: The Economic Growth and Trade Policy Linkages, in Low, P. (ed.), *International Trade and the Environment* (World Bank, Washington D.C.).

Low, P. (ed.) (1992a), *International Trade and the Environment* (World Bank, Washington D.C.).

Low, P. (1992b), Mini Symposium: Trade and the Environment, *World Economy* 15, 101–105.

Low, P. (1992c), International Trade and the Environment: An Overview, in Low, P. (ed.), *International Trade and the Environment* (World Bank, Washington D.C.).

Low, P. and A. Yeats (1992), *Do Dirty Industries Migrate?*, in Low, P. (ed.), *International Trade and the Environment* (World Bank, Washington D.C.).

Lucas, R. (1993), On the Determinants of Direct Foreign Investment: Evidence from East and Southeast Asia, *World Development* 21, 391–406.

Lucas, R., D. Wheeler and H. Hettige (1992), Economic Development, Environmental Regulation and the International Migration of Toxic Industrial Pollution: 1960–1988, in Low, P. (ed.), *International Trade and the Environment* (World Bank, Washington D.C.).

Lutz, E. (1992), Agricultural Trade Liberalisation, Price Changes and Environmental Effects, *Environmental and Resource Economics* 2, 79–89.

Magee, S. and W. Ford (1972), Environmental Pollution, the Terms of Trade and the Balance of Payments, *Kyklos* 25, 101–118.

Maler, K. (1990), International Environmental Problems, *Oxford Review of Economic Policy* 6, 80–108.

Markusen, J. (1975a), International Externalities and Optimum Tax Structures, *Journal of International Economics* 5, 15–29.

Markusen, J. (1975b), Co-operative Control of International Pollution and Common Property Resources, *Quarterly Journal of Economics* 89, 618–632.

Martin, J., J. Burniaux, G. Nicoletti and J. Oliveira Martins (1992), The Costs of International Agreements to Reduce CO_2 Emissions: Evidence from GREEN, *OECD Economic Studies* 19, 93–122.

McGuire, M. (1982), Regulation, Factor Rewards and International Trade, *Journal of Public Economics* 17, 335–354.

Melo, J. de (1988), Computable General Equilibrium Models for Trade Policy Analysis in Developing Countries: A Survey, *Journal of Policy Modelling* 10, 469–503.

Melo, J. de and D. Tarr (1992), *A General Equilibrium Analysis of US Foreign Trade Policy* (MIT Press, Cambridge, Massachusetts).

Merrifield, J. (1989), The Impact of Selected Abatement Strategies on Transnational Pollution, the Terms of Trade and Factor Rewards: A General Equilibrium Approach, *Journal of Environmental Economics and Management* 15, 259–284.

Mikic, M. (1999), Agricultural Trade and Environment: Exploring the Linkages, in Ratnayake, R. (ed.), *Trade and the Environment, A New Zealand Perspective* (Aldershot, Ashgate).

Ministry for the Environment (1994), *Climate Change; The New Zealand Approach* (Ministry for the Environment, Wellington).

Ministry for the Environment (1995), *Environment 2010 Strategy: A Statement of the Government's Strategy on the Environment* (Ministry for the Environment, Wellington).

Ministry of Foreign Affairs and Trade (1993), *New Zealand Trade Policy: Implementation and Directions; A Multi-Track Approach* (Ministry of Foreign Affairs and Trade, Wellington).

New Scientist (1993), *New Zealand's Poisoned Paradise*, July 1993.

Newbery, D. (1990), Acid Rain, *Economic Policy: A European Forum* 5, 297–346.

Nordhaus, W. (1991a), Economic Approaches to Greenhouse Warming, in Dornbusch, R. and J. Poterba (eds.), *Global Warming: Economic Policy Responses* (MIT Press, Cambridge).

Nordhaus, W. (1991b), The Cost of Slowing Climate Change: A Survey, *Energy Journal* 12, 7–65.

Oates, W., K. Palmer and P. Portney (1993), *Environmental Regulation and International Competitiveness: Thinking About the Porter Hypothesis, Resources for the Future*, Working Paper 94-02.

O'Connor, D. (1994), *Managing the Environment with Rapid Industrialisation: Lessons from the East Asian Experience*, OECD Development Centre, Paris.

OECD (1978), *Macroeconomic Evaluation of Environmental Programmes*, OECD, Paris.

OECD (1993), *Environmental Policies and Industrial Competitiveness*, OECD Documents, Paris.

OECD (1994a), *The Environmental Effects of Trade*, Joint Committee on Environment and Trade, Paris.

OECD (1994b), *Life-Cycle Management and Trade*, OECD Documents, Paris.

Palmer, K., W. Oates and P. Portney (1995), Tightening Environmental Standards: The Benefit-Cost of the No-Cost Paradigm, *Journal of Economic Perspectives* 9, 119–132.

Park, I. (1995), *Regional Integration Among the ASEAN Nations: A Computable General Equilibrium Model Study* (Praeger, London).

Parks, R. and J. Cox (1985), The Economic Implications of Log Export Restrictions: Analysis of Existing and Proposed Legislation, in Deacon, R. and M. Johnson (eds.), *Forestlands: Public and Private* (Ballinger, Cambridge).

Pasurka, C. (1985), Environmental Control Costs and United States Effective Rates of Protection, *Public Finance Quarterly* 13, 161–182.

Pearson, C. (1987), *Multinational Corporations, Environment and the Third World* (Duke University Press, Durham).

Perroni, C. and R. Wigle (1992), *International Trade and Environmental Quality: How Important are the Linkages?*, presented at the Annual Canadian Economics Association Meetings.

Perroni, C. and R. Wiggle (1994), International Trade and Environmental Quality: How Important are the Linkages?, *Canadian Journal of Economics* 27, 551–567.

Pethig, R. (1976), Pollution, Welfare and Environmental Policy in the Theory of Comparative Advantage, *Journal of Environmental Economics and Management* 2, 160–179.

Phillips, L. (1974), *Applied Consumption Analysis* (North-Holland, Amsterdam).

Philpott, B. (1992), *General Equilibrium Modelling for Policy Analysis and Economic Planning*, RPEP Occasional Paper 102, Victoria University of Wellington.

Philpott, B. and G. Nana (1993), *A 1990 Inter-Industry Table with Disaggregated Agriculture as the Database for the 1990 Julianne Model*, RPEP Paper 253, Victoria University, Wellington.

Pollack, R. and T. Wales (1981), Demographic Variables in Demand Analysis, *Econometrica* 49, 1533–1551.

Porter, M. (1991), America's Green Strategy, *Science America* 168.

Porter, M. and C. Linde (1995), Towards a New Conception of the Environment-Competitiveness Relationship, *Journal of Economic Perspectives* 9, 97–118.

Radetski, M. (1992), *Economic Growth and Environment*, in Low, P. (ed.), *International Trade and the Environment* (World Bank, Washington D.C.).

Ratnayake, R. (1998), Do Stringent Environmental Regulations Reduce International Competitiveness? Evidence from an Inter-Industry Analysis, *International Journal of the Economics of Business* 5, 77–96.

Ratnayake, R. (ed.) (1999), *Trade and the Environment, A New Zealand Perspective* (Aldershot, Ashgate).

Ratnayake, R. (1999), Trade and Environmental Linkages in Manufacturing Industries, in Ratnayake, R. (ed.), *Trade and the Environment, A New Zealand Perspective* (Aldershot, Ashgate).

Reynolds, R., W. Moore, M. Arthur-Worsop and M. Storey (1993), *Impacts on the Environment of Reduced Agricultural Subsidies: A Case Study of New Zealand*, MAF Policy Technical Paper 93/12 (Ministry of Agriculture and Fisheries, Wellington).

Richardson, J. and J. Mutti (1976), Industrial Development Through Environmental Controls: The International Competitive Aspect, in Walter, I. (ed.), *Studies in International Environmental Economics* (Wiley, New York).

Richardson, J. and J. Mutti (1977), International Competitive Displacement from Environmental Control, *Journal of Environmental Economics and Management* 4, 135–152.

Robertson, D. (1992a), *Trade and the Environment: Harmonisation and Technical Standards*, in Low, P. (ed.), *International Trade and the Environment* (World Bank, Washington D.C.).

Robertson, D. (1992b), *GATT Rules for Emergency Protection*, Thames Essay (Harvester-Wheatsheaf, London).

Robinson, H. (1988), Industrial Pollution Abatement: The Impact on the Balance of Trade, *Canadian Journal of Economics* 21, 187–199.

Runge, C.F. (1994), Environmental Effects of Trade in the Agricultural Sector, in *The Environmental Effects of Trade*, published by the OECD Joint Committee on Environment and Trade, Paris.

Sadafi, R. and P. Low (1992), *International Policy Co-ordination and Environmental Quality*, in Low, P. (ed.), *International Trade and the Environment* (World Bank, Washington D.C.).

Sedjo, R. and C. Wiseman (1983), The Effectiveness of an Export Restriction on Logs, *American Journal of Agricultural Economics* 65, 113–116.

Sharp, B. (1999), Trade and Environmental Linkages in New Zealand Fisheries, in Ratnayake, R. (ed.), *Trade and the Environment, A New Zealand Perspective* (Aldershot, Ashgate).

Shoven, J. and J. Whalley (1984), Applied General Equilibrium Models of Taxation and International Trade, *Journal of Economic Literature* 22, 1007–1051.

Siebert, H. (1977), Environmental Quality and the Gains from Trade, *Kyklos* 30, 657–673.

Siebert, H. (1985), Spatial Aspects of Environmental Economics, in Kneese, A. and J. Sweeney (eds.), *Handbook of Natural Resource and Energy Economics* (North-Holland, New York).

Smith, V. and J. Espinosa (1994), *Environmental and Trade Policies: Some Methodological Lessons*, Working Paper.

Smith, V. and J. Espinosa (1995), Measuring the Environmental Consequences of Trade Policy: A Non-Market CGE Analysis, *Journal of American Agricultural Economics* 77, 772–777.

Solow, A.R. (1991), Is there a Global Warming Problem?, in Dornbush, R. and J.B. Poterba (eds.), *Global Warming: Economic Policy Responses* (MIT Press, Cambridge).

Sorsa, P. (1992), *GATT and the Environment: Basic Issues and Some Developing Country Concerns*, in Low, P. (ed.), *International Trade and the Environment* (World Bank, Washington D.C.).

Sorsa, P. (1994), *Competitiveness and Environmental Standards: Some Exploratory Results*, Policy Research Working Paper, The World Bank.

Srinivasan, T. and J. Whalley (1986), *General Equilibrium Trade Policy Modelling* (MIT Press, Cambridge).

Stroombergen, A. and B. Philpott (1980), *Julianne: A New Zealand General Equilibrium Model Stressing International Trade*, RPEP Occasional Paper 40, Victoria University of Wellington.

Stroombergen, A. and B. Philpott (1981), *The Julianne General Equilibrium Model: A Twenty-Six Sector Version*, RPEP Occasional Paper 48, Victoria University of Wellington.

Subramanian, A. (1992), Trade Measures for the Environment: A Nearly Empty Box?, *The World Economy* 15, 135–152.

Taylor, L. (1993), The World Bank and the Environment: The World Development Report 1992, *World Development* 21(5), 869–881.

Ten Kate, A. and J. Draaisma (1994), *Environment and Economic Growth in Mexico*, processed, Mexico City.

Tobey, J. (1990), The Effects of Domestic Environmental Policies on Patterns of World Trade: An Empirical Test, *Kyklos* 43, 191–209.

Tyler, L. and R. Lattimore (1990), Assistance to Agriculture, in Sandrey, R. and R. Reynolds (eds.) *Farming Without Subsidies* (New Zealand Government Print).

Ugelow, J. (1982), A Survey of Recent Studies on Costs of Pollution Control and the Effects on Trade, in Rubin, S. (ed.), *Environment and Trade* (Allanheld, New Jersey).

United States Department of Commerce (1975), *The Effects of Pollution Abatement on International Trade — III.*

Van Grasstek, C. (1992), The Political Economy of Trade and the Environment in the United States, in Low, P., (ed.), *International Trade and the Environment* (World Bank, Washington D.C.).

Varian, H. (1984), *Microeconomic Analysis* (Norton, New York).

Vasavada, R., U. Saint-Louis and G. Debailleul (1993), The Conflict Between Trade Policy and Environmental Policy in Agriculture, in Shane and Von Witzke (eds.), *The Environment, Government Policies and International Trade: A Proceedings*, ERS, USDA, Staff Report AGES9314, Washington D.C.

Wallace, R. and B. Philpott (1980), *Joanna: A Johansen Type General Equilibrium Model for New Zealand*, RPEP Occasional Paper 43, Victoria University of Wellington.

Walter, I. (1973), The Pollution Content of American Trade, *Western Economic Journal* 11, 61–70.

Walter, I. and J. Ugelow (1979), Environmental Policies in Developing Countries, *Ambio* 8, 102–109.

Whalley, J. (1991), The Interface Between Environmental and Trade Policies, *Economic Journal* 101, 180–189.

Whalley, J. and R. Wigle (1991), Cutting CO_2 Emissions: The Effects of Alternative Policy Approaches, *The Energy Journal* 12, 109–124.

Wheeler, D., and P. Martin (1992), Prices, Policies and the International Diffusion of Clean Technology: The Case of Wood Pulp Production, in Low, P. (ed.), *International Trade and the Environment* (World Bank, Washington D.C.).

Williams, P. (1995), *The Environment, New Zealand as An International Citizen* (MFAT).

Wooding, P. (1987), Liberalising the International Trade Regime, in Bollard, A. and B. Buckle (eds.), *Economic Liberalisation in New Zealand* (Allen Unwin).

Working Group on CO_2 Policy (1996), *Climate Change and CO_2 Policy: A Durable Response* (Ministry for the Environment, Wellington).

World Bank (1992), *World Development Report*, Washington D.C.